Montgomery Bus Boycott

MONTGOMERY BUS BOYCOTT

David Aretha

MORGAN
REYNOLDS
PUBLISHING

Greensboro, North Carolina

THE CIVIL RIGHTS MOVEMENT

The Trial of the Scottsboro Boys

Marching in Birmingham

Selma and the Voting Rights Act

The Murder of Emmett Till

Freedom Summer

Montgomery Bus Boycott

THE CIVIL RIGHTS MOVEMENT:
MONTGOMERY BUS BOYCOTT
Copyright © 2009 by David Aretha

Library of Congress Cataloging-in-Publication Data

Aretha, David.
  Montgomery Bus Boycott / by David Aretha.
    p. cm. -- (Civil rights series)
  Includes bibliographical references and index.
  ISBN-13: 978-1-59935-020-2
  ISBN-10: 1-59935-020-3
  1. Montgomery Bus Boycott, Montgomery, Ala., 1955-1956. 2. Montgomery
(Ala.)--Race relations. 3. Segregation in transportation--Alabama--Montgomery-
-History--20th century. 4. African Americans--Civil rights--Alabama--
Montgomery--History--20th century. I. Title.
  F334.M79N41455 2008
  323.1196'073076147--dc22

                                    2008018679

Printed in the United States of America
First Edition

Contents

A mug shot of Rosa Parks taken during the Montgomery Bus Boycott *(Courtesy of AP Images/Montgomery County Sheriff's Office)*

one

"Are You Going to Stand Up?"

Darkness had settled in when Rosa Parks left the Montgomery Fair Department Store on December 1, 1955. It was 5:30, and the unassuming, forty-two-year-old had just put in a full day as a tailor's assistant. Parks walked to the Court Square bus stop and soon boarded the city bus. She knew not to sit in the first five rows, which by local law were reserved for white passengers. The rear rows belonged to African Americans, and the middle rows were "no man's land." Parks took a seat in row six, next to a black man.

When the bus stopped at the Empire Theater, white people climbed aboard and filled up the first five rows. According to local custom, if the white section was overflowing, black passengers in the middle "no man's land" seats had to stand up so that white people could sit down. At the Empire stop, one white man was left without a seat.

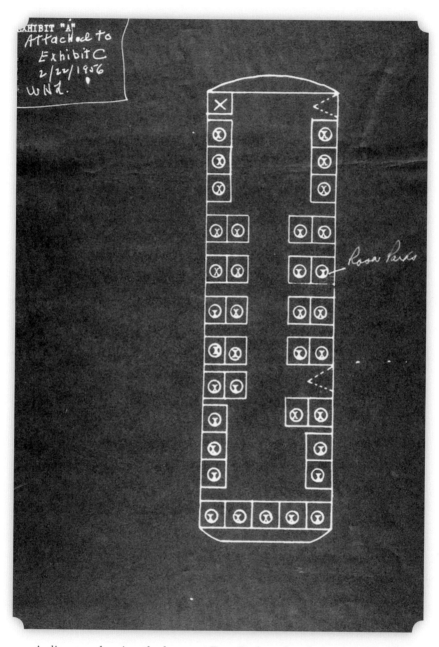

A diagram showing the bus seat Rosa Parks refused to move from on
December 1, 1955 *(Courtesy of National Archives)*

"All right, you folks, I want those two seats," bus driver James F. Blake declared. Blake wanted all four black passengers in row six to stand because, based on custom, a white person shouldn't have to sit in the same row as black people. Nevertheless, none of the four passengers obeyed his first demand. "Y'all better make it light on yourselves and let me have those seats!" Blake ordered.

The two women across the aisle from Parks got up, as did the black man next to her. But Parks didn't. She simply slid over to the window seat. At some point, Parks recognized the driver. Anger rose inside her. It was the same driver who had humiliated her on a city bus twelve years earlier. He was a large man with red hair and a mean look on his face.

Blake had been driving all day and had a busload of passengers. He was in no mood to put up with the stubborn seamstress.

"Look woman, I told you I wanted that seat," he said. "Are you going to stand up?"

Was she going to stand up? Blake was asking more than he realized. For hundreds of years, most black Americans had been afraid to stand up for themselves for fear of whites' reprisals, which were often severe. Now Parks could stand up for herself, and for fellow African Americans, by remaining seated.

"No," Parks said to Blake. "I'm tired of being treated like a second-class citizen."

"If you don't stand up, I'm going to have you arrested," Blake said.

"You can do that," she responded.

Though angry and nervous, Parks remained glued to her seat. As passengers squirmed uneasily, Blake parked the bus and put a call in to his supervisor. The boss told him to call the police, which Blake did. They arrived in a few minutes and arrested the defiant black woman in row six. From that moment on, the city of Montgomery would never be the same.

Within hours, Montgomery's black activists would begin to mimeograph fliers announcing a boycott of the city buses. Almost without exception, Montgomery's African Americans would heed the call. They were tired of being treated like second-class citizens—like something less than human. Ninety-two years after the Emancipation Proclamation, they were still being humiliated on a daily basis—and they were sick of it.

Black Southerners had staged other boycotts in the South, but never one so pervasive, so long-lasting, and so successful. The Montgomery bus boycott thrust Dr. Martin Luther King Jr. into the spotlight and sparked nonviolent black rebellion throughout the South. More than any other episode, the Montgomery boycott triggered the modern civil rights movement. For more than a decade afterward, great numbers of black (and white) activists would hammer away at "Jim Crow" segregation. They would demand to sit wherever they wished in buses, theaters, restaurants, and other public places. They would insist on admittance to public schools and universities. And they would demand that they be allowed to vote—a right denied to a large percentage of black citizens since the days of Reconstruction.

America as we know it changed significantly on December 1, 1955. And it all started with Rosa Parks.

two

Jim Crow's Stranglehold

"Back then, we didn't have any civil rights," Rosa Parks recalled about her childhood in Tuskegee, Alabama. "It was just a matter of survival, of existing from one day to the next. I remember going to sleep as a girl hearing the [Ku Klux] Klan ride at night and hearing a lynching and being afraid the house would burn down."

Born in 1913, Rosa Louise McCauley was fortunate enough to receive a good education. She attended the Montgomery Industrial School for Girls, followed by the Alabama State Teacher's College High School. But life was never easy. When her mother became ill, Rosa had to take care of her.

Rosa married Raymond Parks in 1932, and she graduated high school two years later at age twenty-one. From 1943 to 1957, Parks volunteered with the NAACP, for which her husband also worked. She served as a secretary and later as a youth leader of a local branch. Parks continued volunteering with the NAACP up through 1955. "There were cases of flogging, peonage, murder, and rape," she said. "We didn't seem to have too many successes. It was more a matter of trying to challenge the powers that be, and to let it be known that we did not wish to continue being second-class citizens."

Parks had been humiliated on a Montgomery bus back in 1943. Bus driver James F. Blake—the same driver who would have her arrested in 1955—told her to enter the bus from the rear after she paid her fare. Parks dropped her purse and had the audacity to sit briefly on a "white" seat as she picked it up. As soon as she exited the front door so that she could reenter in the rear, Blake sped off. Parks walked more than five miles to get home—in the rain.

Of course, virtually every African American had suffered physical, mental, and/or economic abuse in the South. This was true not only during the era of slavery (1619-1865) but in all the years leading up to the boycott crisis.

After the Civil War, black Southerners had reason for optimism. In 1865, the Thirteenth Amendment to the U.S. Constitution abolished slavery and involuntary servitude. And in 1870, the Fifteenth Amendment guaranteed voting rights to all adult male citizens. But southern whites fiercely resisted these changes, before and after Federal troops left the South in 1877. Beginning in 1865, legislatures in the former Confederate states enacted "black codes." African Americans could not serve on juries, bear arms, rent land, assemble together (except for church), drink alcohol, travel, or even learn to read. In 1866, the Ku Klux Klan, an underground organization devoted to white supremacy, was formed in Pulaski, Tennessee.

Whites understood that they had to suppress the black vote in order to maintain their political power. (In some counties,

THE FIFTEENTH AMENDMENT.
CELEBRATED MAY 19T 1870.

Illustrations of the rights granted to African Americans by the Fifteenth Amendment *(Library of Congress)*

the number of black citizens exceeded the number of whites.) Thus, southern legislatures devised many schemes to prevent African Americans from voting. They initiated expensive poll taxes, forced blacks to prove their literacy, and made voting-registration applicants pass difficult civics tests to "earn" the right to vote. If all else failed, they fired, assaulted, and sometimes killed black Americans who tried to vote.

With virtually no good options available, large numbers of former slaves remained on southern plantations. Typically, they picked cotton for long hours, often in oppressive heat, for pitiful wages. Black sharecroppers, those who rented

Members of the Ku Klux Klan in 1948 *(Library of Congress)*

farmland from whites, immediately fell into debts that they couldn't possibly repay. Thus, economically at least, they were still enslaved.

As in the days of slavery, the South remained segregated. "Jim Crow," originally a minstrel character from the 1830s, became a euphemism for segregation in the South. In the Jim Crow system, two separate societies existed: one for whites and an inferior one for blacks. Whites preferred the system for several reasons. They could devote more tax dollars to white facilities (such as schools) and less to black facilities. Through separate restrooms, drinking fountains, park benches, movie houses, etc., they could avoid coming in contact with the "inferior" race, which many whites even considered subhuman.

A police officer stands at a train depot with a sign set up to enforce segregation. *(Courtesy of AP Images)*

Moreover, segregation would help prevent the white man's ultimate fear—sexual intercourse between black men and white women. Nothing infuriated white men more than the thought of a "black buck" impregnating a "white maiden" and producing a "mongrel" child. In the South, at least one law was created to prevent "reckless eyeballing," meaning a black man could not even look at an attractive white woman. Over the years, hundreds of black men were lynched because they allegedly had associated with white women.

Buses didn't exist in the late 1800s, but trains did. And legislators made sure that blacks did not share seats and rub shoulders with members of the white race. In 1870, Tennessee passed the first transportation segregation law, which mandated the separation of black and white passengers on trains. In the 1880s, multiple southern states separated the races to a greater extent, as they mandated that railroad companies provide separate rail cars for black passengers.

In the late 1800s, whites had the U.S. Supreme Court on their side. In *Louisville, New Orleans and Texas Railway Company v. Mississippi,* the Supreme Court permitted states to segregate public transportation facilities. In *Plessy v. Ferguson* (1896), the U.S. Supreme Court ruled that it was constitutional for governments to maintain separate facilities for black and white citizens as long as the facilities were "equal." For the next half-century, the "equal" part was rarely enforced. Black facilities were seemingly always inferior. As late as the 1960s, the state of Mississippi spent four times more money educating a white student than a black pupil.

Discrimination carried over to the workforce. Relatively few black Southerners made a decent salary or wage. Socially, many whites talked down to blacks—a carryover from the master/slave relationship from a hundred years earlier. Whites called a black man "boy," and blacks had to call a white man "Mister." Even in the Montgomery phone book, white women were referred to as "Mrs." or "Miss" while black women were granted no such courtesy.

The cumulative humiliations had profound effects on black Americans. In a 1940s study, social psychologist Kenneth Clark found that most black children when given a choice preferred a white doll to a black one. Even at an early age, the children had deducted that blacks were inferior to whites. This notion was perpetuated throughout the Jim Crow South, resulting in low self-esteem and self-defeatism among black Americans.

Some African Americans, though, mustered the courage to fight the system. In Nashville in 1905—fifty years before the Montgomery boycott — black citizens boycotted the city's newly segregated streetcars. Declared Reverend J. A. Jones, "[T]he day the separate streetcar law goes into effect . . . that day the company will lose nine-tenths of its negro patronage. [T]he self-respecting, intelligent colored citizens of Nashville will not stand for Jim Crowism on the streetcar lines in this city." The boycott petered out when the company began experiencing mechanical problems.

Some people had success, albeit limited, in fighting segregation and injustice. Around the turn of the century, Ida B. Wells edited a newspaper, *Free Speech,* which reported harrowing facts about lynching. In 1909, black rights leader W. E. B. DuBois helped found the National Association for the Advancement of Colored People (NAACP). Its members promised to "secure for all people the rights guaranteed in the 13th, 14th, and 15th amendments to the United States Constitution, which promised an end to slavery, the equal protection of the law, and universal adult male suffrage, respectively." The NAACP also launched an anti-lynching campaign. Moreover, behind the heroic efforts of attorneys

W. E. B. DuBois *(Library of Congress)*

Charles Houston and Thurgood Marshall, the organization also tried to overturn segregation laws in the courts, particularly in schools.

Other great civil rights leaders preceded Rosa Parks and Martin Luther King Jr. In the 1910s, Marcus Garvey launched a bold initiative to send black Americans to Liberia in Africa, where they could govern themselves. In New York in the 1930s, Adam Clayton Powell railed against discrimination and police brutality in his newspaper column. He led black New Yorkers in protests against employment discrimination, and he participated in the "Don't Buy Where You Can't Work" campaign. In 1941, labor leader A. Philip Randolph planned a march on Washington to protest racial discrimination in war industries. The threat prompted President Franklin Roosevelt to issue the Fair Employment Act, which stated that companies working with the federal government could not discriminate against any race or ethnicity when hiring workers.

The civil rights movement stagnated during the Great Depression and World War II. Although black Americans suffered worst of all during the Depression, white America endured its own hardships and had little sympathy for the black cause. During the war, many southern African Americans migrated to northern cities to take manufacturing jobs, and thousands of black soldiers served in the war.

After the war, white America became somewhat more accepting of African Americans. Millions cheered for Jackie Robinson when he broke Major League Baseball's color barrier in 1947. A year later, President Harry Truman issued an executive order that ended segregation in the military. Lynchings declined, and federal judges began to rule against segregated schooling. In 1950, for example, the U.S. Supreme

Court ruled that black students had the right to attend white graduate schools.

Nevertheless, Jim Crow still ruled in the South, particularly in Mississippi and Alabama. "In the whole state of Alabama we had probably less than five black doctors," said Reverend Ralph Abernathy, talking about the mid-1950s. "You had a restroom for white males and a restroom for white women, and you had a restroom for colored. Meaning that colored people had to use the same restroom, male and female. And the janitor never would clean up the restroom for the colored people."

Two episodes that resonate with the Montgomery bus boycott occurred during this era. In 1944, Irene Morgan, age twenty-seven, boarded a Greyhound bus in Virginia to see a doctor in Baltimore. The young mother sat in the designated "colored" section, but when more white passengers boarded, the driver told her to move farther back. When she said no, the sheriff was called. Morgan tore up the arrest warrant and was dragged, kicking and screaming, off the bus.

Morgan appealed her conviction (for violating Virginia's segregation law), and the case went all the way to the U.S. Supreme Court. Attorney Thurgood Marshall argued that segregation on interstate travel was an improper burden on commerce, and the justices agreed. In subsequent years, attorneys would use the court's ruling to try to desegregate public services.

If Morgan was the Rosa Parks of Virginia, then Reverend T. J. Jemison was the Martin Luther King Jr. of Baton Rouge, Louisiana. In 1953, Jemison led a bus boycott in that city. Baton Rouge had an ordinance that called for first-come, first-serve seating on the city buses. When white bus drivers refused to follow the law, Jemison started the boycott. Black citizens even created their own amateur taxi service—a predecessor of the one used in Montgomery. In fact, Jemison and King were friends (Jemison called him Mike), and during the Montgomery boycott King sought Jemison's advice about how to run a volunteer taxi system.

On May 17, 1954, the U.S. Supreme Court dropped a bombshell on the South. In *Brown v. Board of Education of Topeka,* the High Court ruled that segregation in public schools was unconstitutional. Southern whites were outraged, believing that northern agitators were out to destroy the southern way of life. As President Dwight Eisenhower said privately to Chief Justice Earl Warren, Southerners were "concerned lest their sweet little girls be seated alongside some big black bucks."

Southern whites worried not just about the end of segregated schooling but the demise of Jim Crow segregation in general. They feared they would have to share swimming pools, restrooms, drinking fountains, and bus seats with African Americans. Declared the *Jackson Daily News,* "White and Negro children in the same schools will lead to miscegenation [sex between members of different races]. Miscegenation leads to mixed marriages and mixed marriages lead to mongrelization of the human race."

While some school districts (notably those in Baltimore and Washington, D.C.) would desegregate their schools by 1955, most southern governments resisted. In fact, southern whites railed against integration more strongly than ever. White Citizens' Councils sprang up throughout the South. Their mission: to use economic pressure to keep African Americans off the voting rolls and to maintain segregation. Due to the circumstances, black Southerners were flush with anger. The Supreme Court had just granted them a long-overdue right, and now the whites of their communities were taking that precious right away. It was in this tension-filled atmosphere that the Montgomery bus boycott would emerge.

In the summer of 1955, a horrible crime was committed in Mississippi that also had an impact on Montgomery.

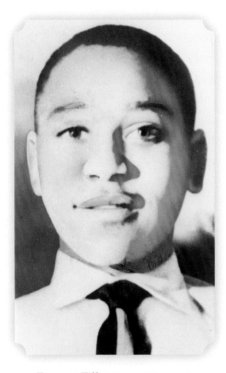

Emmett Till *(Library of Congress)*

African American Emmett Till, a fourteen-year-old free-spirit from Chicago, flirted with white Carolyn Bryant in a rural grocery store. Bryant's husband, Roy Bryant, and his half-brother, J. W. Milam, responded by fatally beating and shooting Till. Moreover, an all-white jury let them off scot-free. The story infuriated blacks and whites throughout the country, including those in Montgomery.

Said Mamie Bradley, Till's mother: "The black people of Montgomery were outraged and determined following Emmett's murder when Dr. King led the bus boycott there. They were moved by it." The Till case also inspired Rosa Parks to take her stand against segregation. "Someone asked Rosa Parks why she didn't get up when she was threatened," Reverend Jesse Jackson said. "She said she thought about Emmett Till, and couldn't go back anymore."

U.S. Senate Apologizes over Lynchings

In 2005, the U.S. Senate apologized for spending decades blocking anti-lynching bills from becoming law. Nearly 5,000 Americans—mostly black males—were lynched between 1882 and 1960. Some two hundred anti-lynching bills were introduced in Congress during the first half of the twentieth century, and seven presidents petitioned Congress to end lynching. But the Senate repeatedly stopped any such efforts. If lynching had been made a federal crime, the legislation would have allowed the federal government to prosecute those responsible. As it was, 99 percent of all perpetrators of lynching escaped punishment by either state or local officials, many of whom were often complicit in the crimes.

Ida B. Wells-Barnett *(Courtesy of R. Gates/Hulton Archive/Getty Images)*

One of the most passionate and effective lobbyists against lynching was Ida B. Wells-Barnett, a teacher and journalist who once wrote that "eternal vigilance is the price of liberty." Initially motivated by the 1892 lynching in Memphis of three black businessmen, Wells-Barnett spent decades writing newspaper columns, pamphlets, and other investigative works to try to force the government to enact anti-lynching legislation. She didn't live to see the change she fought so hard to attain, but seventy-five years after her death, at least one of her descendants was there to witness the Senate apology—her grandson Troy Duster, a professor of sociology at New York University and the University of California at Berkeley.

three
Primed for
Protest

It was the Saturday before Christmas in 1949, and Jo Ann Robinson "had never felt freer or happier." Robinson, an upbeat African American English teacher from Georgia, had just finished her first semester of teaching at Alabama State College (ASC) in Montgomery. She had enjoyed the camaraderie of the ASC staff and the enthusiasm of her students. Now she was off to Ohio for a vacation with family and friends.

On Saturday morning, Robinson climbed aboard a Montgomery bus, which she would take to a friend's house; from there they would drive to the airport. She paid her fare in the near-empty bus and took a seat in the fifth row. Suddenly, the driver stopped the bus. In a harsh tone, he yelled something at Robinson; she couldn't understand. He then got out of his seat, walked toward her, and raised his hand as if he was going to smack her.

Downtown Montgomery, Alabama, in the late '50s.

"Get up from there!" he scolded. Scared stiff, Robinson didn't move. "Get up from there!" he yelled again.

Panicked, Robinson bolted toward the front door—forgetting momentarily that black riders were supposed to exit through the rear. Shaken and humiliated, she sobbed heavy tears.

"My friends came and took me to the airport, but my holiday season was spoiled," Robinson wrote. "I cried all the way to my destination and pretended to have a headache when my relatives met me at the airport in Cleveland five or six hours later. In all these years I have never forgotten the shame, the hurt, of that experience. The memory will not go away."

In her brief but indelible encounter, Robinson had experienced the shame that African Americans had felt in

Montgomery for more than a century. Founded in 1819, the city had always been segregated—its African Americans always oppressed. In fact, after southern states began seceding from the Union in 1860, Montgomery became the capital of the Confederate States of America. The order to attack Fort Sumter, triggering the Civil War, was issued from Montgomery.

After Reconstruction, Jim Crow gripped Montgomery as tightly as any other southern city. In 1886 Montgomery became the first city in the nation to install electric streetcars, but public transportation remained segregated for the next seventy years. The whole city was segregated. Some African Americans made decent livings as doctors, teachers, businessmen, and so on, but they were the exception. Most black men worked as laborers or in service jobs, while most black women toiled as maids in white people's homes. Moreover, whites made considerably more money than blacks, even if their jobs were the same.

Well into the 1950s, the city's 70,000 whites had greater rights on the Montgomery City Lines than did the city's 50,000 black citizens. According to the law, a bus's front ten seats (two seats in each of the front five rows) were reserved for white passengers. Black riders were designated the rear seats, and the middle seats were dubbed "no-man's land." About three-quarters of Montgomery's bus riders were African American, but troubles arose when a large number of whites joined them on the bus. Once whites filled up the front ten seats, the remaining whites were entitled to the seats behind those ten. Black passengers in those middle rows had to give up their seats to the white riders—even if the black passengers were elderly, pregnant, or physically impaired. Often, the black passengers would have to stand for the duration of their

A segregated bus with white passengers in the front seats and African American passengers in the back *(Courtesy of Stan Wayman/Time Life Pictures/ Getty Images)*

ride. If African Americans did not leave these seats voluntarily, the bus driver would demand that they do so, sometimes adding such pejoratives as "nigger" or "whore."

The front ten seats were also an issue. If a bus was crammed with black passengers—with not a single white person on board—the riders still could not sit in the ten empty "white" seats. It didn't matter if they were juggling packages or trying to comfort a baby.

Montgomery featured segregated schools, restaurants, restrooms, and drinking fountains. But black citizens felt the pain of segregation most acutely on the buses. Whites were right there, in their faces. Blacks had to swallow whatever pride they had and cower subserviently to the back of the bus. In addition, the buses were confining and the weather was often hot, creating stifling conditions.

"Before the boycott, we were stuffed in the back of the bus just like cattle," remembered Gussie Nesbitt, a domestic worker. "I work hard all day, and I had to stand up all the way home, because I couldn't have a seat on the bus. And if you sit down on the bus, the bus driver would say, 'Let me have that seat, nigger.'"

The seating policy was one of many injustices that black bus riders endured. White neighborhoods had more bus stops, meaning blacks had to walk greater distances to get to their stop. The Montgomery City Lines employed only white drivers, despite the many routes through all-black neighborhoods.

Many of the bus drivers were courteous to all passengers, but many others harassed black riders. Some drivers slammed the door in the faces of late-arriving riders, unwilling to wait even a second or two. Some drivers didn't hand change and transfers at black passengers, but instead threw the coins or paper at them. If a rider didn't have the exact fare, the driver might not give him or her any change back. On rainy days, some drivers refused to let African Americans on the buses. When African Americans boarded the bus, they had to pay in the front, step outside, and enter through the rear door. If a driver was in a particularly bad mood, he might take off before the passenger made his or her way to the rear door.

According to Robinson, such humiliation deeply affected passengers. "The Women's Political Council, over a long period, tried to ascertain why there was so much killing, cutting, intoxication, and burglary, etc., on weekends among black children and adults," she wrote. "We discovered that all the pent-up emotions resulting from bitter experiences on local transportation lines often were released upon husbands, wives, or children, resulting in injuries that necessitated hospital care."

After years of humiliation on the buses, many black passengers stewed in anger. Said one black maid about a driver, "I got mad and I put my hand on my razor. I looked at him and told him, '…if you so bad, git up outta that seat.' I rode four blocks, then I went up to the front door and backed off the bus, and I was jest hoping he'd git up. I was going to cut his head slamp off, but he didn't say nothing."

Of course, few black passengers talked that way to the bus drivers, for they understood the consequences. In 1950, a black soldier named Thomas Edward Brooks quarreled with his driver about his bus fare. The driver called the police, who shot Brooks dead as he walked off the bus. Three years later, a driver refused to accept a transfer from passenger Epsie Worthy and demanded that she pay ten cents for an additional fare. Refusing to pay, Worthy left the bus. But the driver, who wouldn't let it die, went after her and beat her with his hands. Worthy, who fought back, was arrested, convicted, and fined for disorderly conduct.

Beginning in 1946, women in Montgomery fought back in a more sophisticated manner. That year, a courageous scholar named Mary Fair Burks helped start the Women's Political Council (WPC), a group comprised mostly of educators at Alabama State College (an all-black school) and Montgomery's black public schools. During its first few years, the WPC—with Burks as president—focused on getting African Americans registered to vote. Members opened schools to teach black citizens how to fill out registration forms and pass literacy tests.

In 1950, when Jo Ann Robinson became president of the organization, the WPC began to focus on the bus situation in Montgomery. WPC leaders received numerous complaints from bus riders, and on multiple occasions they discussed these issues with the three commissioners of Montgomery, including Mayor W. A. Gayle. Robinson and her staff denounced the segregation rules and asked for black drivers and more bus stops in black neighborhoods. The mayor was always pleasant and seemingly sincere in his willingness to improve conditions. Yet Gayle and the city never made any improvements.

WPC leaders also met with officials of the Montgomery City Lines, which ran the buses. The company did agree to add more bus stops in black neighborhoods, but it refused to budge on the other issues. Segregation, the company spokesmen stated, was the law, and there was nothing they could do about it.

Robinson, still haunted by her experience on the city buses, could not tolerate such inaction. Shortly after the *Brown v. Board of Education* decision in May 1954, Robinson penned a bold letter to the mayor. "Mayor Gayle," she wrote, "three quarters of the riders of these public conveyances are Negroes. If Negroes did not patronize them they could not possibly operate . . . there has been talk from 25 or more local organizations of planning a city-wide boycott of buses."

Of course, it was a lot easier to talk about a boycott than actually staging one. Black citizens, most of whom couldn't afford cars, depended on the buses to get to work. Worse, they could be harassed, arrested, or fired from their jobs for staging a protest. A few years earlier, a bus driver told Reverend Vernon Johns to get up from his seat so that a white man could sit down. When Johns asked fellow African Americans to leave the bus with him, no one did. "You ought to have knowed better," one of them told him.

Still, the black activists of Montgomery were determined to challenge the Jim Crow bus system. E. D. Nixon, president of the Progressive Democratic Association (PDA), was the most prominent activist of all. In 1940, he had led hundreds of African Americans to a Montgomery County courthouse, demanding to be registered to vote. In subsequent years, the deep-voiced, captivating speaker became a respected local leader on the issue of human rights. Whenever black citizens were arrested for violating a "race" law, they could call Nixon to bail them out of jail or find them a lawyer. Yet despite Nixon's influence, he and the PDA failed in their attempts to meet with the bus company.

Fortunately for African Americans, a few local ministers were able to arrange a conference with the City Commission. One of these preachers was Reverend Martin Luther King Jr., the twenty-six-year-old pastor of Montgomery's Dexter Avenue Baptist Church. King, who had graduated with a B.A. in sociology from Morehouse College at age nineteen, also had earned a Bachelor of Divinity degree from Crozer Theological Seminary. His brilliance shone through in his eloquent sermons of love, compassion, and the need to battle racial injustice.

King and the ministers, along with three women of the WPC, met with the city commissioners. The WPC submitted complaints, which the commissioners promised to investigate. Afterward, more dialogue opportunities opened up. At a public hearing regarding a proposed increase in bus fares, WPC representatives submitted a list of complaints. They included obscene language and name-calling by bus drivers; bus stops that were too spaced out in black neighborhoods; the humiliating and dangerous practice of black riders having to enter the rear door; and the reserving of ten double seats in the front (out of thirty-six total) for white passengers.

Martin Luther King Jr. *(Library of Congress)*

Robinson and other WPC members also got to speak with J. H. Bagley, manager of the Montgomery City Lines. Bagley said he couldn't do anything to change the segregation laws. The WPC women also met with Mayor Gayle, who treated them graciously. The very next day, black riders were pleasantly surprised to see buses stop at every block in their neighborhoods. Drivers, too, seemed more courteous than usual.

"But the joy was short-lived," Robinson recalled. "The mumblings started again, as stories of unhappy experiences began to circulate once more." On a particularly frigid day, a black passenger asked the driver to turn up the heat. The driver responded by opening the doors to let the cold air blow in while he drove. When a mentally challenged black man walked in front of a bus, the driver responded by beating him severely. His punishment: a $25 fine plus court costs.

One day, a black woman with two infants entered a bus. In order to search her pocketbook for change, she placed the babies on one of the front seats. The driver demanded that she get the "black, dirty brats" off the seat—then stepped on the accelerator, causing the babies to fall to the floor.

Something had to be done. But first, a particular incident would have to occur. If a black passenger were arrested— and the incident were publicized—it might rally the masses. Moreover, they could use the case to challenge the bus segregation laws in the courts.

Besides Nixon and the WPC, Clifford Durr and Fred Gray were ready for action. Durr, a white Alabama-born attorney, had for years defended individuals whose civil liberties had been violated. He had worked in President Franklin Roosevelt's administration, and he was a friend of future president Lyndon Johnson. In 1955, Durr worked

1956 picture of Attorney Fred Gray (*Courtesy of Don Cravens/Time Life Pictures/Getty Images*)

in Montgomery defending black citizens who were victims of the Jim Crow system. Durr worked with young African American attorney Fred Gray. Just one year out of school, the quiet but determined Gray's ambition had been "to become a lawyer, return to Alabama, and destroy everything segregated I could find."

On March 2, 1955, an incident occurred that aroused Durr's and Gray's interest. While picking up white passengers on Dexter Avenue, the bus driver noticed that they had no place to sit. The ten white seats had already been filled, and black passengers had filled up the back of the bus as well as the middle "no man's land" seats—those reserved for neither blacks nor whites. Operating within custom, the driver asked four black women in a middle row to get up so that the new white passengers could sit down. Two did, but the two other women refused.

The driver asked again, but when they refused he hailed a nearby police officer. Three policemen soon boarded the bus. Trying to avoid arrest, the officers asked black men to give up their seats for the two obstinate black women. Just one man did, but the remaining female resistor remained in her seat. She was a feisty fifteen-year-old named Claudette Colvin. At one point during the incident, Colvin declared: "I done paid my dime. I ain't got no reason to move."

Since she refused to cooperate, the police arrested Colvin. She cried and then screamed when the officers slapped on the handcuffs. Prosecutors charged Colvin with violating the bus segregation law, assault, and disorderly conduct. Montgomery's black citizens, after reading about the case in the newspaper, were steamed. Colvin was just a high school student, and besides, sitting in "no man's land" did not technically violate the segregation law.

Nixon moved first on the case. He arranged a meeting with Police Commissioner Dave Birmingham, Martin Luther King Jr., and others. Whites at the meeting did not object to the black reps' request: that drivers be courteous to all passengers and that a new policy be instituted—with whites filling up the front of the bus and blacks the rear. The drivers could not kick black riders out of the "no man's land." However, Jack Crenshaw, attorney for the bus company, squelched the agreement. He said it violated the existing law.

On May 6, Judge Eugene Carter found Colvin guilty of only one charge, assault, which according to witnesses was preposterous. Nixon wanted to appeal the case, but he eventually decided not to. He realized it would be hard to fight against Montgomery's segregation law now that she was no longer accused of violating it. Moreover, it was revealed that Colvin was pregnant. It would be virtually impossible to rally support around a "sinful" young woman.

By the fall of 1955, some black citizens had already stopped riding the Montgomery buses. They preferred to walk than to deal with all the tension and humiliation. In October, Mary Louise Smith was also arrested for refusing to yield her seat. Again, Montgomery's black activists prepared to challenge the system. But Nixon decided not to proceed. Smith lived in a clapboard shack, and her father was an alcoholic. Nixon felt that the lawyers needed a victim with great character and a clean background to build their case around. That person was Rosa Parks.

Parks said that many thoughts swirled through her mind as she sat defiantly on the bus on December 1, waiting for the police to arrive. "People always say that I didn't give up my seat because I was tired, but that isn't true," Parks wrote. "I was not tired physically, or no more tired than I usually was at the end of a working day. I was not old, although some people have an image of me as being old then. I was forty-two. No, the only tired I was, was tired of giving in."

As the police officer arrested Parks, she asked him: "Why do you push us all around?"

"I don't know," the officer responded, "but the law's the law, and you're under arrest."

With that, the officer drove Parks to the police station. From that point on, Parks' life—and the future of America— would change dramatically.

four

The Boycott Begins

That night, Rosa Parks was taken to the city jail. Officers booked and fingerprinted her and locked her in a cell. Allowed a phone call, Parks called her mother, Leona, who asked if the police had beaten her—which was not uncommon in Alabama at the time. Leona then phoned E. D. Nixon's wife, who called her husband at his downtown office.

Understanding that Parks needed a lawyer, Nixon tried to reach black attorney Fred Gray but couldn't track him down. He called the city jail, but the police refused to answer his questions. Nixon then phoned white attorney Clifford Durr (a friend of Parks), who got those at the city jail to talk. Parks, they told him, had been arrested for violating Alabama's segregation laws.

Durr, his wife, Virginia, and Nixon all drove to the city jail. They released Parks on bond and drove her home, where

POLICE DEPARTMENT
CITY OF MONTGOMERY

Date 12-1-55 19___

Complainant   J.F.Blake   (wm)

Address   27 No.Lewis St.

Phone No.

Offense   Misc.

Reported By   Same as above

Address

Phone No.

Date and Time Offense Committed   12-1-55   6:06 pm

Place of Occurrence   In Front of Empire Theatre   (On Montgomery Street)

Person or Property Attacked

How Attacked

Person Wanted

Value of Property Stolen   Value Recovered

Details of Complaint (list, describe and give value of property stolen)

We received a call upon arrival the bus operator said he had a colored female

sitting in the white section of the bus, and would not move back.

We (Day & Mixon) also saw her.

The bus operator signed a warrant for her. Rosa Parks, (cf) 634 Cleveland Court.

Rosa Parks (cf) was charged with chapter 6 section 11 of the Montgomery City Code.

Warrant #14254

THIS OFFENSE IS DECLARED:
UNFOUNDED ☐
CLEARED BY ARREST ☐
EXCEPTIONALLY CLEARED ☐
INACTIVE (NOT CLEARED) ☐

Officers   F. B. Day

D.W. Mixon

Division   Patrol

Time 7:00 pm
12-1-55

The police report filed on the night Parks was arrested (*Courtesy of National Archives*) her much-relieved husband, Raymond, and mother greeted her. Out of earshot from the Parks family, Clifford Durr and Nixon began to talk about using the Parks case to challenge bus segregation in the courts. Had they decided not to act, the world might never have heard about Rosa Parks or, perhaps, Martin Luther King. But they pushed the issue. Parks, they thought, was the ideal candidate. She was humble and dignified with a spotless record.

Nixon pulled Rosa aside and asked her if she would fight the case with them. He recalled: "I ended up by saying to her point-blank, 'Mrs. Parks, with your permission we can break down segregation on the bus with your case. If I wasn't convinced that we can do it, I wouldn't bother you by it.'"

As a longtime member of the NAACP, Parks understood the magnitude of such an undertaking. Rosa talked first to her mother and then her husband, who at one point was totally against it. "Oh, the white folks will kill you, Rosa," he told her. "Don't do anything to make trouble, Rosa. Don't bring a suit. The whites will kill you."

But Rosa didn't listen to her husband. "If you think it will mean something to Montgomery and do some good, I'll be happy to go along with it," she said. And with that, Nixon went home and made an announcement to his wife: "Baby, we're going to boycott the Montgomery buses."

That very night, Montgomery's black activists went to work. Fred Gray, after retrieving Nixon's messages, called members of the Women's Political Council, including WPC President Jo Ann Robinson. The women met at their offices at Alabama State. Wasting no time, they crafted a letter calling for a boycott of Montgomery's buses on Monday, December 5. Using the school's mimeograph machines, they produced some 50,000 leaflets before the sun rose on Friday.

The letter read, in part:

> Another Negro woman has been arrested and thrown in jail because she refused to get up out of her seat on the bus for a white person to sit down. . . . If we do not do something to stop these arrests, they will continue. The next time it may be you, or your daughter, or mother. . . . We are, therefore, asking every Negro to stay off the buses Monday in protest of the arrest and trial. Don't ride the buses to work, to town, to school, or anywhere. . . . You can . . . afford to stay out of town for one day. If you work, take a cab, or walk. But please, children and grown-ups, don't ride the bus. . . .

Robinson took charge of distributing the leaflets, which would be tricky since if white authorities discovered what she was doing, she could be arrested and her leaflets confiscated. From four to seven o'clock that morning, Robinson and two of her Alabama State students plotted the routes on which they would distribute the leaflets—routes that the WPC had planned a while back. Avoiding drawing suspicion, Robinson taught her eight o'clock class as scheduled. After that, she and her two young accomplices hopped in their cars and began their historic mission.

The trio dropped off large bundles of leaflets at strategic locations. Other WPC members arranged to have those bundles delivered to schools, businesses, factories, beauty parlors—wherever Montgomery's black citizens congregated in large numbers. No one seemed to know the authors of the letter, but everyone knew that this was a big deal. On Friday, just one day after Rosa Parks' arrest, Montgomery's black community was abuzz about the planned bus boycott.

Like Robinson, Nixon also worked through the wee hours of Friday morning. He needed to work quickly because, as a railroad porter, he had to leave town later that morning. Nixon phoned some of the city's prominent black ministers, including King, and asked them to arrange a meeting of ministers that afternoon. Nixon asked King if they could meet at King's church, the Dexter Avenue Baptist Church, because of its central location. King obliged.

Before leaving on a train bound for Atlanta, Nixon made an audacious call to Joe Azbell, city editor for the *Montgomery Advertiser*. Nixon told him that if he wanted a hot story, he should meet him at the train station. There, after Azbell promised him anonymity, Nixon filled him in on all the developments. With the pamphlets, the upcoming news story, and the ministers' Sunday sermons, virtually everyone in Montgomery would know about the boycott.

On Friday afternoon and evening, dozens of ministers and other black community leaders met in the basement of Dexter Avenue Baptist Church. As a group, they supported the boycott, thus taking an unprecedented stance against Montgomery's white establishment.

These leaders spent the rest of the day trying to facilitate the upcoming protest. A smaller committee within the group, including King, drafted a shorter boycott announcement that they mimeographed right there at Dexter. "Don't ride the bus to work, to town, to school, or any place Monday, December 5," the letter stated. "If you work, take a cab, or share a ride, or walk." The new letter welcomed black citizens to attend a mass meeting at the Holt Street Baptist Church (the largest black church in Montgomery) at 7 p.m. on Monday, the day of the boycott.

Those at the Friday meeting also tried to organize the one-day boycott as best as they could. Alfonso Campbell was selected to head the transportation committee. Cars would have to follow the bus routes on Monday to give rides to boycotting bus passengers. The committee members called the city's eighteen black taxi companies, encouraging them to be heroic during Monday's crazy rush hours.

The Dexter meeting lasted until about midnight, and on Saturday the upcoming boycott was the talk of the town. The story made the Saturday afternoon edition of Montgomery's *Alabama Journal,* one day before the *Advertiser* article was printed. The local television and radio stations also blared the news during the weekend. The WPC had hoped against hope that black citizens would have kept the boycott secret in order to shock the white establishment on Monday. But now the city leaders, the police, and the bus company had

King discusses boycott strategies with other boycott organizers on January 27, 1956. *(Courtesy of Don Cravens/Time Life Pictures/Getty Images)*

advance notice, which put blacks on edge. With their sermons on Sunday, black preachers encouraged their congregations to have strength and persevere.

Monday, December 5, 1955, ranks among the most seminal days in African American history. In anticipation, Coretta King—along with her husband, Martin— awoke before dawn. She waited anxiously next to her front window, looking for the first bus of the morning to roll past. They knew that the first bus would be telling, since it was typically packed with black domestic workers.

The previous night, Martin and Coretta had agreed that a 60-percent boycott rate would be a success. But when that first morning bus rumbled up past the Kings' house, Coretta couldn't believe her eyes. "I was in the kitchen drinking my coffee," King wrote, "when I heard Coretta cry, 'Martin, Martin, come quickly!' I put down my cup and ran toward the living room. As I approached the front window Coretta pointed joyfully to a slowly moving bus: 'Darling, it's empty!' I could hardly believe what I saw."

King continued: "Eagerly we waited for the next bus. In fifteen minutes it rolled down the street, and, like the first, it was empty. A third bus appeared, and it too was empty of all but two white passengers."

King hopped in his car and drove around the city. At some point he realized that the all-white police force had accidentally contributed to the success of the boycott. Over the weekend, rumors had flown that hundreds of domestics had phoned their white employers. Reportedly, they said that they would have to miss work on Monday because they were afraid to ride the buses.

As often happened in the Jim Crow South, whites misinterpreted blacks' intentions and motivations. Police

An empty bus in Montgomery during the boycott *(Courtesy of AP Images)*

Commissioner Clyde Sellers had deducted that black protesters would be at the bus stops forcing other blacks to stay off the buses. As Joe Azbell's front-page story stated on Monday morning: "Negro 'goon squads' reportedly have been organized here to intimidate Negroes who ride Montgomery City Line buses today."

In response, Sellers assigned two motorcycle policemen to follow every bus. His intentions seemed honorable: to prevent intimidation and violence and to allow those blacks who wanted to ride the buses to do so. But Sellers' plan turned out to be completely counterproductive. First, no "goon squads" existed at any of the stops. As it turned out, it was the presence of motorcycle policemen who intimidated the black citizens. Those who had intended to board the buses got one look at the men in blue and wanted no part of the whole situation. Instead, they walked, took a taxi, or accepted a ride from the many black drivers who had volunteered on this special day.

The boycott was a phenomenal success. The number of blacks riding buses was down more than 90 percent on Monday. Many carpooled to work and school. Some even rode mules and horse and buggies. Some white employers, out of either empathy or pragmatism, picked up their black workers. Among those who walked to their destinations, spirits ran high. They sang songs and cheered the empty buses as they rolled past.

Such responses irritated many of the bus drivers, who interpreted the cheers as jeers. Drivers complained to police that schoolchildren had stuck out their tongues at them as they drove by. Some kids did indeed taunt the drivers. "You wanted your buses, now you got 'em," they cried. Nevertheless, the boycott went off without any serious incidents. Only one person was arrested: a college student who had offered an old black woman a ride in his car.

The one-day boycott put the bus company on notice. Since at least three-quarters of the city's regular bus riders were black, bus revenue dropped dramatically on Monday. Many of the white riders had skipped riding the bus that day, either in support of the boycotters or to avoid the whole scene. Moreover, downtown merchants complained about the lack of black customers on Monday. African Americans had neither the means of transportation nor the desire to go Christmas shopping on that momentous day.

Meanwhile, Monday was also Parks's day in court. This, too, developed into a big event. In the morning, she was convicted of disorderly conduct and fined $10 (and charged $4 for court costs). Immediately, attorney Fred Gray filed notice of appeal—the first step in his challenge of the segregation laws.

Rosa Parks (left), E. D. Nixon (middle), and Fred Gray appear in court on Dec. 5, 1955, to file a notice of appeal against Rosa's conviction. *(Courtesy of AP Images)*

As E. D. Nixon walked out of the courtroom to post bond for Parks's release, he couldn't believe what he saw. Some five hundred black citizens had arrived to show their support. The massive crowd filled the halls and extended down the courthouse steps and into the street. Nixon grew anxious by the restlessness of the crowd and the armed guards who tried to contain them. Some crowd members threatened to storm the courthouse if Parks wasn't released immediately. Fortunately, this episode also ended peacefully.

King speaks to a crowd during a mass meeting at the Holt Street Baptist Church. *(Courtesy of AP Images/Gene Herrick)*

Extraordinary events continued to unfold on Monday. In the afternoon, ministers and other black leaders gathered at Holt Street Baptist Church to prepare for the 7 o'clock meeting. Due to the success of the boycott, those in attendance realized that they now had great bargaining power with the city leaders. A prolonged boycott would devastate the bus company and downtown merchants.

Working from this strength, Nixon, Reverend Ralph Abernathy, and a Methodist minister put together a list of boycott demands. Some members of the larger group suggested that the list be mimeographed and passed to the masses at

Ralph Abernathy *(Courtesy of Don Cravens/Time Life Pictures/Getty Images)*

that night's meeting. They didn't want the demands to be discussed for fear that white reporters would make them public. Another suggested that the names of the boycott's leaders be concealed. At that point, Nixon rose to his feet and demanded that the ministers not act so cowardly. Black maids had shown their bravery that morning by staying off the buses; now it was time for Montgomery's men of the cloth to show their courage.

Reverend King arrived at the meeting in the middle of Nixon's diatribe. "Brother Nixon, I'm not a coward," King announced. King declared that all the boycott leaders should reveal their names.

But just who would be the leaders of the boycott—and specifically, *the* leader? Shortly after King's comment, longtime voting-rights activist Rufus Lewis—who happened to be a member of King's Dexter church—rose to nominate his pastor as president of this new group. Lewis may have made the suggestion so that Nixon, whom he never much liked, wouldn't rise to the top. After some discussion, no one else was nominated, so King was the new president.

Over the years, historians have speculated as to why the black leaders agreed to select King. Some say that his great character and oratory skills made him an ideal candidate. Others say that he hadn't been in the city long enough (just fifteen months) to make any enemies. In addition, no one else seemed to want the position. Only the bravest of men would, and as King had said, "I'm not a coward."

Those at the meeting then selected a name for the new organization: the Montgomery Improvement Association (MIA). Other officers were also selected. They included Nixon as treasurer and Reverend L. Roy Bennett and Dr. Moses W. Jones as vice presidents. For a time, everyone debated whether they should continue the boycott or suspend it during the negotiations. The consensus was to suspend it, for if they continued the boycott and it eventually fell apart, they no longer would have a negotiating weapon. Nevertheless, they ran out of time before they could reach a conclusion.

At dinner time King rushed home, but he had no time to chat with Coretta or play with his baby, Yolanda. He had just minutes to prepare his speech for the 7 o'clock mass meeting. Little did he realize how much thinking time he'd have on the ride back to Holt, due to a massive traffic jam. Anywhere from 5,000 to 15,000 African Americans were descending on the church, which could hold only a fraction of that total. King arrived to see the amplifiers that would broadcast his speech to those who couldn't squeeze their way into the church.

Most of those in attendance were unfamiliar with King. But as he addressed the multitudes, he soon discovered that they were on his side. Early in his speech, he talked about democracy, the oppression of African Americans, and Rosa Parks, with the audience punctuating his words with "yes," "amen," and "that's right."

Then, more than four hundred words into the speech, King struck a chord. "And you know, my friends," he said, "there comes a time when people get tired of being trampled over by the iron feet of oppression." This time, the massive crowd erupted in applause, as if he had just expressed the precise sentiment they had felt their entire lives. The applause did not diminish but instead grew louder, with the cheers from outside rumbling like thunder. People stomped on the wooden floors until the entire building shook.

Inspired now, King maintained the momentum. "There comes a time, my friends, when people get tired of being plunged across the abyss of humiliation, where they experience the bleakness of nagging despair. There comes a time when people get tired of being pushed out of the glittering sunlight of life's July, and left standing amid the piercing chill of an alpine November. There comes a time." A deafening roar filled the building. King declared that it was time for the black citizens of Montgomery to stand up for themselves. "Now let us say that we are not here advocating violence," he said. "The only weapon that we have in our hands this evening is the weapon of protest. . . . My friends, I want it to be known that we're going to work with grim and bold determination to gain justice on the buses in this city."

King continued:

> We are not wrong in what we are doing. If we are wrong, the Supreme Court of this nation is wrong. If we are wrong, God Almighty is wrong! If we are wrong, Jesus of Nazareth was merely a utopian dreamer that never came down to earth. If we are wrong, justice is a lie. . . . And we are determined here in Montgomery to work and fight until justice runs down like water, and righteousness like a mighty stream.

Again, applause ripped through the Holt Street church. By the time he finished his speech, the blacks of Montgomery were committed to boycott until justice prevailed. And for the first time in city history, they had a black leader to rally around: a twenty-six-year-old pastor who, just a few hours earlier, had just been another guy at a meeting. Recalled Donie Jones, "Reverend King prayed so that night, I'm telling you the . . . truth, you had to hold people to keep them from getting to him."

After King spoke, the crowd was asked if they wanted to end the boycott after just the one day. "No" was the seemingly unanimous response. One person shouted that it was only the beginning, which was affirmed by tremendous applause. Reverend Ralph Abernathy announced the demands of the boycott to the crowd, which were reported in the *Alabama Journal* the next day. The four-part resolution urged:

> 1) That all citizens of Montgomery, regardless of race, refrain from riding the buses of the City Lines Bus Company until arrangement was agreed upon between citizens and that company.
> 2) That vehicle owners would give free rides to others during the boycott.
> 3) That employers of workers who lived far away try to provide transportation for them.
> 4) That Montgomery's black citizens were prepared and willing to send a delegation to the bus company to work out a solution.

The MIA's initial demands were modest. They sought three things: better courtesy from the white drivers, the hiring of black drivers for black neighborhoods, and a new seating system. According to their proposal, whites would fill up the front seats and black the rear seats. The seating would be "first come, first served," meaning the driver could not kick black riders out of the middle seats to make room for a white patron, and black riders wouldn't have to stand when a seat was vacant. Such a system had worked fine in Mobile, Alabama, and other southern cities. Why not Montgomery?

The WPC and NAACP did not consider these demands strong enough. They wanted the buses to be fully integrated so that black riders could be treated like first-class citizens and sit wherever they wanted to. Although Robinson and the WPC urged King to demand full integration, they loyally supported the MIA's positions.

The boycott continued on Tuesday, December 6, as neither the MIA nor the city commissioners attempted to seek reconciliation. The bus company's spokesman, a fidgety lawyer named James Crenshaw, deflected responsibility for the troubles on the buses. He talked only about the segregation law and how the company was obliged to obey it. But for Crenshaw, the real issue wasn't about law or protecting a private company's rights. It was about maintaining white power. He revealed his true colors when he said, "If we granted the Negroes these demands, they would go about boasting of a victory that they had won over the white people, and this we will not stand for."

The company's manager, the kindly J. H. Bagley, suggested to the commissioners to give the "first-come" system a try since it worked well in Mobile. But the three commissioners—W. A. Gayle (the mayor), Clyde Sellers (the police commissioner), and Frank Parks—were steadfastly against the plan. They did not explain their reasoning, but certainly they did not want to show that they were giving in to the upstart activists. Throughout the South in 1955 (in reaction to the *Brown* decision), more whites were taking a stand against integration than supporting it.

On December 7, Reverend Robert E. Hughes stepped forward to bring the two sides together. Hughes was the white executive director of the Alabama Council on Human Relations (ACHR), whose purpose was to improve race relations in the state. The ACHR was able to get the city commissioners, bus company officials, and black leaders together for a morning meeting on Thursday, December 8.

At the meeting, King verbalized the MIA's three demands: first-come, first serve; black drivers; and better courtesy. On all three points, Crenshaw refused to budge. He said that the seating was illegal, no one could tell the bus company whom to hire, and the drivers already were courteous. Five hours of talking led nowhere, and the meeting ended without anything being solved. Diplomacy had failed; it was time for war.

five

Breakdowns

S hortly after the bus boycott began, Montgomery's white establishment's effort to defeat the strike became self-destructive. On December 8, the *Alabama Journal* reported that, according to police, four buses had been shot at, presumably by African Americans. But no one was arrested or suspected, and the alleged evidence seemed far-fetched. For example, in one such incident, police said that the shooting came from a two-story house, yet the only such house on the block was owned by a white family.

Montgomery City Lines also made some baffling decisions. Though overall bus revenue was down about 75 percent, the company gave drivers a raise (in order to divert a strike). The company also suspended service in certain black neighborhoods. This meant that many African Americans couldn't ride the buses even if they wanted to. Thus, the bus company was perpetuating the boycott.

The MIA scheduled mass meetings for every Monday and Thursday evening in order to keep citizens informed, accept donations, and bolster morale. At the first Thursday night meeting, on December 8, Martin Luther King Jr. had to ask citizens to sacrifice even further. Earlier in the day, Commissioner Sellers had hinted that Montgomery's two hundred-plus cab drivers could face heavy fines if they did not charge each passenger the minimum fare, which was forty-five cents. King knew that without a fleet of taxis, the boycott would be in trouble. Thus, he asked for volunteers—those who would volunteer their time and/or their cars.

At first, the relatively few black car owners were reluctant to donate their prize possessions. But many ministers agreed to do it, as did members of the WPC. Scores of people volunteered. Irene West, who was in her seventies, would transport people in her Cadillac day after day.

As it turned out, the boycott relied heavily on the volunteers because the police came down hard on the real taxi drivers. They enforced the forty-five cent fare and forced drivers to bring their cabs in for checkups. The MIA created a Transportation Committee, headed by Alfonso Campbell and Rufus Lewis, to plan routes and oversee the private taxi service. The committee designated more than forty dispatch stations, such as black churches, and about the same number of pickup areas.

Each day, beginning at 5 a.m., more than three hundred vehicles transported black citizens to work. Because some domestics got off work in the early afternoon, the dispatch drivers began at 1 p.m.—and continued until 8. Two downtown locations served as main hubs: the parking lot of a black woman and the commercial property of Dr. Richard Harris, a black pharmacist. Due to so much come-and-go, business at Harris' pharmacy boomed.

Boycotters carpooling as an empty bus sits nearby *(Courtesy of Don Cravens/ Time Life Pictures/Getty Images)*

The volunteer drivers gassed up for free at the eight black-owned service stations in Montgomery. The service station managers then billed the MIA, which paid the huge gas bills with the money it collected at meetings. Only two problems remained: an overall financial strain on the black protesters, and the physical demands on the volunteer drivers. Many volunteers were spending time before and after work shuttling people to and fro.

Fortunately for Montgomery's black citizens, word of their efforts had spread throughout the nation and generous donations poured in. People donated not only money—which the MIA used to pay its debts and bills—but also vehicles.

Eventually, the MIA operated a small fleet of station wagons, and it even had the money to pay people to drive them. Montgomery's volunteer transportation system worked beautifully. Even the local pro-segregationist White Citizens' Council admitted that it operated with military precision.

The boycott even inspired some of Montgomery's white population. Juliette Morgan, a white librarian known for her deep knowledge of history, was one of the few liberal-minded whites who spoke out. On December 12, Morgan wrote a letter in the *Montgomery Advertiser.* Praising the boycotters, she wrote: "The Negroes of Montgomery seem to have taken a lesson from Gandhi. . . . One feels that history is being made in Montgomery these days. . . . It is hard to imagine a soul so

The fleet of station wagons operated by the MIA for carpooling *(Courtesy of Don Cravens/Time Life Pictures/Getty Images)*

dead, a heart so hard, a vision so blinded and provincial as not to be moved with admiration at the quiet dignity, discipline and dedication with which the Negroes have conducted their boycott."

Morgan continued to write to the *Advertiser,* prompting whites to harass her with threatening phone calls. Mayor W. A. Gayle even insisted that the library fire her. Her superiors didn't, but they demanded that she stop her letter writing.

Meanwhile, Mayor Gayle had bigger problems: The boycott was killing the bus company and downtown merchants. He scheduled a meeting for Saturday, December 17 that seemed to represent everyone involved: the three commissioners, black leaders, lawyers, and bus company officials as well as representatives from the Merchants Association, PTA, Chamber of Commerce, Ministerial Union, labor unions, and even the White Citizens' Council. Gayle also invited two prominent black business owners who were notorious "yes" men, P. M. Blair and Dungee Caffey; they'd do seemingly anything the mayor asked of them. After three hours, this unwieldy assembly made no progress.

Gayle decided to reduce the committee to eleven people— eight whites and three blacks, including Blair and Caffey. King demanded equal representation, and Gayle finally agreed to eight representatives of each race. In the end, it was all for naught. The two sides, black versus white, argued for the rest of the meeting and throughout the follow-up meeting on Monday. The white committee refused to bow to any of the black leaders' demands. At one point, a white woman who was serving as the meeting's secretary lashed out at King. She was the first white person to support the hiring of black drivers because, she said in anger, "black men were used as white people's chauffeurs."

Montgomery Mayor W. A. Gayle *(Courtesy of Don Cravens/Time Life Pictures/ Getty Images)*

At the conclusion of the fruitless meeting, the eight white members submitted recommendations to the city commissioners. The most significant, but confusing, recommendation included reserve seating up front for whites; the number of reserve seats would be decided by each driver and would depend on the average patronage of each race on his route. Since the black committee members didn't agree to any of the recommendations, they were in essence meaningless.

More than ever, the boycotters were on their own. The MIA tried to bolster morale at the twice-weekly meetings. At one meeting, a preacher told the story of an elderly woman named Mother Pollard, who now walked to her destinations. "My feets is tired, but my soul is rested," said Pollard. That line would be repeated throughout the civil rights movement whenever a group marched for freedom.

Meanwhile, Christmas sales dropped significantly at downtown stores. Black citizens had neither the ease of transportation nor the inclination to go shopping. These were not normal times. Few African Americans felt like making special arrangements to get downtown only to give their precious few dollars to white merchants. King urged people to put their Christmas money in their savings account and in the coffers of the MIA. The bus company struck its own blow against the downtown merchants by canceling *all* bus service in the city from December 22 through 25. Company officials felt they might as will give the bus drivers a few days off, especially since revenue was so minimal.

On Christmas Day, the MIA ran an ad in the Montgomery newspapers, stating the purpose of its boycott and discussing the need for people to get along. These words were picked up by numerous newspapers and disseminated all over the world. But as the spirit of Christmas flamed out and the

January winds whipped through Montgomery, kind hearts turned cold.

Harsh reality hit the city commissioners during the first week of the new year. The bus company insisted that it had to raise fares due to the lack of riders. The commissioners reluctantly conceded, even though they knew that the rate hike would hurt them at the ballot box.

Police Commissioner Sellers, however, was determined to place the blame on the troublemakers who had started the boycott. Not long after the fare increase was approved, Sellers (and 1,200 others) attended a rally sponsored by the White Citizens' Council, who critics derided as a "white-collar KKK." Members were talking about how to legally retaliate against the black businessmen, such as denying them credit and refusing to sell them supplies for their businesses. Sellers won a roar of approval when he declared to the gathering that he himself was joining the WCC. "In effect," the *Montgomery Advertiser* reported, "the Montgomery police force is now an arm of the White Citizens Council."

Sellers' announcement, of course, troubled the boycotters, who also were suffering from their own exhaustion. Black citizens were growing weary of the daily grind, and the Transportation Committee was struggling to maintain its volunteer fleet. MIA leaders asked for and received a meeting with the three commissioners, and on January 9 attorney Fred Gray presented the trio with a new proposal. Gray conceded that, as a general rule, blacks would sit in the back and whites in the front. However, he insisted on two things: that blacks could sit in the ten front white seats if they were empty and that drivers could not order blacks to vacate the middle rows.

Gray also said that blacks and whites would re-segregate themselves. For example, say a bus is completely full, with four white people in the very front and everyone else black. At the next stop, two whites enter the bus and two blacks get off. In this scenario, two blacks sitting at the front would get up and take the just-vacated rear seats, leaving their seats for the new whites. Similarly, he said, whites would voluntarily move closer to the front if the black section of the bus got too crowded. The commissioners, however, found the whole plan preposterous, especially the part about whites having to get up to make room for black passengers. The meeting ended without any progress made.

Talking to out-of-town black reporters, King insisted that the MIA's resolve was not weakening. He reminded them that the negotiations were separate from the Rosa Parks' case. Her conviction was being appealed, he said, adding, "We are fighting the question of segregation in the courts." To keep spirits up, King announced that mass meetings would be held six days a week.

Often in the Jim Crow South, fear, anger, and misperceptions produced dangerous situations. Such a phenomenon occurred in Montgomery in mid-January. On the 19th, the *Montgomery Advertiser* published an in-depth feature story about King headlined "The Rev. King Is Boycott Boss." Though the article was written objectively, many white readers interpreted King as an elitist outsider with ulterior motives: he and other Negro leaders were using their people as pawns to fulfill their grand agenda—to dismantle segregation in the South and end the southern way of life.

Tensions increased considerably in mid-January. King received an average of thirty-five hate letters a day, many signed "KKK." Reverend Robert Graetz, known around the city as the white pastor of a black church, had his car vandalized. Commissioners Sellers stirred passions even further when he announced that the great majority of the black bus riders did not favor the boycott. They were being forced off the buses, he said, by the goons of the Negro elite. In this highly charged atmosphere, those whites who gave their black employees rides came up with excuses for their empathetic behavior. Some said they were merely protecting their employee from the black goons that Sellers had talked about.

Black protesters also lied to whites about their involvement in the boycott. Virginia Durr overheard a black woman falsely say that none of her family was involved in the boycott. Durr, who was friendly with the woman, asked her why she had lied. "Well, you know," the woman responded, "when you have your hand in the lion's mouth, the best thing to do is pat it on the head."

The boycott story took a bizarre turn on Saturday, January 21. That evening, the Associated Press wired a story about the boycott to its news outlets. The story stated that the city commissioners had met that day with three black ministers, who had agreed to end the boycott without gaining any concessions. When reporter Carl Rowan of the *Minneapolis Tribune* called King to confirm the story, MLK was dumbfounded. King in turn called the *Advertiser* staff, who told him that the story had been released by the city commissioner's office, and would appear in the *Advertiser* the next day.

King soon discovered that the three black ministers were Reverends Kinds and Moseley and Bishop Rice—leaders of small congregations. They had been asked to meet with city officials to discuss insurance. When they arrived at the meeting, the three clergymen refused to discuss the boycott. Nevertheless, the commissioners released the "settlement" story, all of which had been completely fabricated.

The commissioners' attempt to throw the boycott into disarray completely backfired. By Sunday, black leaders and common citizens spread the word that the story had been a hoax, and that the boycott was still on. Angry at the white men's lie, boycotters bonded together. They were more resolved than ever to continue their protest.

Embarrassed by the debacle, Mayor Gayle lashed out. He joined Sellers in the White Citizens' Council and announced the end of biracial meetings. He declared that there would be "no more discussions between the whites and the Negroes until the latter were ready to end the boycott. . . . We have pussyfooted around with this boycott long enough."

The reason black citizens had staged the boycott was to be treated with dignity on the buses. But to Mayor Gayle, the boycotters were the aggressors and whites the victims. "[T]here seems to be a belief on the part of the Negroes that they have the white people hemmed up in a corner and they are not going to give an inch until they can force the white people of our community to submit to their demands—in fact, swallow all of them."

Gayle demanded that whites cease giving rides to their black maids. He also lashed out at those who had been giving their workers an extra dollar per week to pay for whatever extra transportation costs they might have incurred. While many white citizens ignored Gayle's bold statements, many others showered his office with congratulatory telegrams, letters, and phone calls. Gayle's angry rhetoric had inspired whites so much that White Citizens' Council membership quickly skyrocketed.

Beginning in late January, the police force increased itsefforts to break the back of the boycott. From morning to evening, day after day, police pulled over black carpool drivers for alleged moving violations. Black citizens were ticketed for speeding, not slowing down enough at a yield sign, or carrying too many riders in the front seat. Officers handed out tickets like fliers. Despite her best efforts to obey the rules of the road, Jo Ann Robinson was ticketed seventeen times. Dozens of others were arrested and jailed for moving violations. The MIA reimbursed volunteer drivers for their fines, but as tickets mounted the MIA's treasury dwindled. Many worried that their licenses would be suspended or their insurance canceled because they had accrued too many tickets.

On the afternoon of January 26, police landed the big fish. As King was giving boycotters a ride, a motorcycle policeman pulled him over. "Get out, King," the officer demanded. "You're under arrest for speeding thirty miles an hour in a twenty-five mile zone."

At first, terror shook his bones as a squad car carried him on unfamiliar roads, out of the city. Would he, like Emmett Till and so many other "uppity niggers" be taken to the country, lynched, and dumped in a river? King finally breathed a sigh of relief when they pulled into the Montgomery City Jail. He had never been arrested before, and he hadn't known that the jail was on Montgomery's outskirts.

As King was locked in jail, where he chatted with curious cellmates, his wife and his close friend, Reverend Ralph Abernathy, drove frantically to the scene. So, too, did hundreds of King's followers. While Abernathy struggled in vain to put together bond money, the jailers—fearing a mob scene—let King out on his own recognizance. King made it back in time to attend a scheduled mass meeting. At the church, the crowd overflowed so much that the people were told that a follow-up mass meeting would be held at a second church that night. Amazingly, the overflow from that crowd

Montgomery police officers attempted to end the boycott by ticketing African American drivers for alleged moving violations. *(Courtesy of Don Cravens/Time Life Pictures/Getty Images)*

spawned a third meeting—and then a fourth. Incredibly, *seven* mass meetings were held that night, all because of people's love for Martin Luther King Jr.

Yet for King, the pressures were starting to mount. The tickets and arrests were wreaking havoc on black citizens, who bombarded him with complaints. On January 27, he was awakened by a phone call—an angry white man making a vague but ominous threat. King couldn't handle this anymore. He stayed up late pondering whether he should abandon the leadership of the boycott. He prayed to God. "I have nothing left," he said. "I've come to the point where I can't face it alone."

At that moment, King wrote, he felt divine inspiration. "It seemed as though I could hear the quiet assurance of an inner voice saying: 'Stand up for righteousness; stand up for the truth; and God will be at your side forever.' Almost at once my fears began to go. My uncertainty disappeared. I was ready to face anything."

While King found his inner peace, the common folk battled daily stresses. Many of the laid-off bus drivers had been deputized as policemen. Their job: pull over and harass the black taxi drivers. These officers examined the driver's papers and vehicle, and they sometimes demanded that the cars be inspected by a mechanic. Montgomery's mechanics often charged outrageous sums.

Emboldened by the mayor's post-hoax declaration, whites vented their hostilities against the boycotters. White drivers not only insulted black pedestrians, they pelted them with food and other objects as well. White teenagers squirted them with water from balloons. Some even filled the balloons with their urine and sprayed adults and children. Many white citizens purchased Confederate flag stickers for their cars as a symbol of white Southerners' pride and solidarity. Whites routinely harassed black leaders with threatening phone calls. Black citizens generally restrained themselves, but they sometimes retaliated. In one instance, black youths chucked bricks at white youths who had stopped at a traffic light.

On January 30, a frightening incident rocked Montgomery. In the evening, while King was away at a meeting, a white man got out of his car and tossed a bomb onto King's front porch, then sped off. The explosion destroyed the porch, blew

King urges a crowd to remain calm from the front porch of his home after it was firebombed on the night of January 30, 1956. *(Courtesy of AP Images)*

out the front window, and shocked and terrified King's wife and daughter, who were otherwise unharmed. Within minutes, hundreds of people—mostly angry African Americans—rushed to the scene. King, who learned of the bombing but was unsure if Coretta and the baby were hurt, raced home in a panic.

As the crowd grew larger and angrier, police on the scene became nervous for their own safety. Somehow, King mustered the strength to calm the crowd. "Don't get panicky," he said. "Don't get your weapons. . . . We are not advocating violence. We want to love our enemies."

After King spoke, Sellers and Gayle addressed the masses, saying they did not condone violence and promising to find the culprit. Those in the crowd questioned the men's sincerity. Many walked home with tears in their eyes and anger in their hearts.

The Safe Bus Company

African Americans in a North Carolina city found a way to circumvent the Jim Crow laws on the buses: they formed their own bus company. The Safe Bus Company, which operated in the city of Winston-Salem from 1926 to 1972, was formed by a group of blacks who owned small buses called jitneys. The company's name stems from a promise made to Winston-Salem mayor Thomas Barber to operate a safe and organized bus system. Initially, the bus company only provided service from east Winston-Salem, where most blacks lived, to R. J. Reynolds Tobacco Company plants. Electric trolleys and other forms of public transportation did not operate in or near East Winston. However, by 1968 the company had expanded operations to cover the entire city, with a fleet of thirty-five buses. For many years Safe Bus was the only African American-owned city bus company in the nation to run a fixed route for the general public. Eventually, the company was bought by the Winston-Salem Transit Authority, as a means to expand integrated bus service.

six

Battles in the Courts

Since the boycott began, hard-line black activists had urged lawyers to file a lawsuit against Montgomery. They disagreed with the MIA's tame requests for better courtesy and rearranged seating on the buses. They wanted the city's bus segregation laws to be abolished—period.

Over the first few weeks of the boycott, lawyers refrained from filing the lawsuit because of fear of reprisals. But with police and white citizens already harassing the boycotters, the attorneys felt it was time to take legal action. The bombing of Martin Luther King's home was the last straw. The next day, on January 31, 1956, five black citizens authorized black attorney Fred Gray to file a lawsuit on their behalf. Clifford Durr and Charles Langford would assist him. On February 1, they filed the papers in a U.S. district court.

Two of the five plaintiffs were familiar: Claudette Colvin

and Mary Louise Smith, who had been arrested on the city buses in 1955. Aurelia Browder, a widowed mother of six, and Susie McDonald, a widowed housekeeper, were other plaintiffs. Browder, a seamstress, was known for not taking any lip from bullying bus drivers. McDonald, a blue-eyed and fair-skinned black woman, had often been told not to sit in the black section of the bus. Jeanatta Reese, a black domestic, rounded out the quintet.

The lawsuit, *Browder* v. *Gayle,* named the three city commissioners as defendants. The suit had three demands:

> 1) The court declare the city's segregation laws unconstitutional, null, and void.
> 2) The court order a speedy hearing and enter an injunction that would restrain each defendant from enforcing laws that compel black citizens (by intimidation, harassment, etc.) to ride the city buses.
> 3) That an injunction be issued to prevent the defendants (and their agents or employees) from using force, threats, etc., to prevent black citizens from using privately provided transportation.

Seemingly in response to the lawsuit, the commissioners halted the harassment of carpoolers. Instead, the vengeance became much more discreet and sinister. On the night of February 1, someone detonated a bomb in E. D. Nixon's backyard. Whites, many of whom were police officers or dressed as officers, attacked black people's homes. According to WPC President Jo Ann Robinson, black civilians accused white policemen of "demolition of automobiles parked in front of houses; spraying yards to destroy beautiful flowers; throwing paint on homes, necessitating new paint jobs; throwing nails in paths of automobiles, causing the tires to puncture; even throwing human manure on porches."

As the boycott dragged on, African Americans were harassed more and more. An African American woman glances over her shoulder at members of the Ku Klux Klan. *(Courtesy of AP Images)*

Police seemed to target the boycott leaders. About two weeks after her picture window was smashed, Robinson noticed two policemen scattering something on her car. It turned out to be acid, which burned large holes in the metal.

February was filled with bad news. On February 7, whites scored a victory at the University of Alabama. Three days after Autherine Lucy was admitted as the first black student in the school's 126-year history, white students assaulted her with rocks, eggs, and tomatoes. The school suspended Lucy "for her own safety." Later, when she tried to fight the suspension, the school expelled her.

On the day of Lucy's suspension, whites retaliated against Gray by changing his draft status. Formerly exempt from serving in the military because he was a minister, Gray was now classified 1-A. This meant he was among the group of American men most likely to be drafted into military service. Three days later, on February 10, the Alabama and Mississippi White Citizens' Councils staged a rally at the Montgomery Coliseum. Attendees applauded city officials for fighting bus desegregation. Speaking to some 10,000 people, U.S. Senator James Eastland of Mississippi urged whites to fight against integration by organizing and being militant.

Black citizens continued the boycott, but white pressure was merciless. On February 13, Circuit Judge Eugene Carter responded to calls for a grand jury investigation of the bus boycott. Carter instructed a grand jury to see whether the protesters were violating a state boycott conspiracy law. Alabama did have such a law. Anyone who staged a boycott without a just cause or legal excuse for so doing was guilty of a misdemeanor. The Montgomery County grand jury included eighteen members—seventeen whites and one black man, waiter E. T. Sinclair, who spent his days serving whites at the Montgomery Country Club.

Around this time, Jeanatta Reese got cold feet, saying she no longer wanted to be a plaintiff in Fred Gray's federal lawsuit. Reese even testified in front of the grand jury, which used her statements to go after Gray. The grand jury indicted him on the charge that he represented clients without authority. Gray was arrested and faced possible disbarment.

The grand jury seemed to take on monstrous proportions. It subpoenaed dozens of members of the bus boycott, from ministers and MIA secretaries to taxi drivers and gas station operators. Moreover, the grand jury was authorized to decide if boycott leaders should be arrested. Those heavily involved with the MIA and WPC feared they would wind up in jail.

Meanwhile, at three different points in February, black leaders met with the Men of Montgomery (MOM). The white businessmen who comprised this organization were tired of losing money, and they staged sincere talks with Martin Luther King Jr. and his colleagues. The black members compromised by saying they would accept reserved seating for white people as long as it was only five seats and not ten. However, they insisted that black drivers be hired for black bus routes; that black passengers be admitted through the front door; and that bus fare be reduced to ten cents, as it had been before the boycott.

In the third meeting, MOM members made its own concessions. African Americans could enter the front door, they said, and the fare would be reduced to ten cents if patronage of the buses increased to sufficient levels. However, they did not accept the hiring of black drivers or the reduction of reserved seats to five. They also offered this concession: "Whenever the condition exists that there is no possibility of any additional

King speaks to the executive board of the Montgomery Improvement Association in 1956. *(Courtesy of AP Images)*

white passengers boarding the bus . . . the bus operator shall assign such seats as may be required in the reserved section." In other words, if seats were empty in the white section and black passengers were standing, the driver could tell the black passengers that they could sit in the white seats.

On February 20, several thousand boycotters attended a mass meeting to vote on this proposal. The few who wanted to accept it were roundly booed. The masses voted to reject the offer and to continue the boycott. As they left the meeting, people were buoyed by pride—determined to forge ahead.

The exhilaration carried over to the next day, when the grand jury made a major announcement. It had determined that the boycott was illegal, and that dozens of black boycott leaders were to be arrested by the following morning. According to Robinson, those who expected to be arrested feared not. "We just took the news as a joke, a pretense, an excitement for the moment. . . . They were defiant, willing to go to jail, ready to let Americans and the world know that they could not and would not take any more."

On the morning of February 22, police arrested the ministers and took them to jail. The ministers then read the list of the other indicted citizens and phoned them, telling them to come down on their own. Fittingly, those with cars picked up those without vehicles and carpooled to the county jail. Attorneys were on hand to bail out everyone, so after they were fingerprinted and processed, they got to go home.

On the rainy morning of February 24, eighty-nine indicted men and women, including Rosa Parks, arrived at the Montgomery County Courthouse for arraignment. Their friends and family joined them, packing the courthouse. Judge Carter set a trial date for King, March 19, which would precede all other trials. Afterward, people walked to King's Dexter Avenue Baptist Church, where they sang, prayed, and listened to the words of their preachers.

Montgomery's white establishment did not seek national publicity, but it indirectly created it with its mass indictments and trial date for King. Media from all over the country flocked to Montgomery. They reported on the scope and success of the boycott, the audacious retaliation by the police, and the charismatic leadership of King. Speculation ran rampant about the upcoming trial. Would King actually be sent to jail? Could black citizens really be convicted for simply

When the courts ruled that the boycott was illegal, many boycott leaders were arrested, including Rosa Parks. *(Library of Congress)*

choosing not to ride the buses? Would the cases be appealed to higher courts?

The big day arrived on March 22. King was found guilty of violating the state boycott law. However, Judge Carter sentenced him to a mere fine, $500 (plus court costs), because King had promoted nonviolence. He was released on bond. Outside the courthouse, black citizens rejoiced. "Long live the king!" and "No more buses!" they shouted. With cameras clicking, Coretta King smooched her smiling husband on the cheek. "I knew that I was a convicted criminal," King would write, "but I was proud of my crime . . . the

King receives a kiss from his wife, Coretta, outside the Montgomery courthouse after only being fined $500 for violating the state boycott law. *(Courtesy of AP Images/Gene Herrick)*

crime of joining my people in a nonviolent protest against injustice."

By trial's end, the boycotters had become American heroes and King was a national sensation. When he traveled to New York for his first northern fund-raiser, some 10,000 people swarmed the Gardner Taylor's Concord Baptist Church and contributed $4,000 to the MIA's fund. On March 28, African Americans in southern and a few non-southern cities honored a National Deliverance Day of Prayer in support of the bus boycott.

By this point, it seemed that the city commissioners had tired of punishing the boycotters. Trial dates for the remaining eighty-eight indicted citizens were never set. Ticketing, arrests, harassment, and attacks all greatly diminished. Meanwhile, leaders of the Montgomery City Lines were feeling the pressure more than ever. Their parent company, National City Lines of Chicago, wanted them to reach a compromise. But Montgomery city commissioners wanted no compromise, and Montgomery City Lines leaders felt they had to kowtow to the city commission; if they didn't, the city might not renew its license.

As for the boycotters, they still had to deal with their initial problem: reaching their destinations without buses. Maintaining the volunteer taxi service was expensive, but fortunately donations poured in from the boycotters themselves and from supporters across the world. Still, the long walks and volunteer hours continued to drain the boycotters, physically and emotionally. It would only get worse during the long, sweltering summer.

In the spring of 1956, a succession of court rulings rocked Montgomery. First, on April 23, the U.S. Supreme Court dismissed an appeal of a federal appeals court ruling that had outlawed bus segregation in South Carolina. This decision was widely misinterpreted as meaning that all intrastate bus segregation was unconstitutional. After the April 23 ruling, bus companies in more than a dozen southern cities decided to end segregated seating on their buses. Most startling, the Montgomery City Lines also decided to implement a policy of desegregation. However, Montgomery commissioners quickly nipped that in the bud. Mayor Gayle announced that bus segregation would continue, and police threatened to arrest bus drivers who disobeyed segregation laws. In early

May, Montgomery officials got an injunction from a state judge that forced the Montgomery bus company to comply with segregation laws.

But for the boycotters, hope was not lost. On May 11, a three-judge federal court listened to arguments in the *Browder v. Gayle* case. Fred Gray, who had avoided disbarment, represented the four remaining plaintiffs, each of whom testified. Circuit Judge Richard T. Rives and district judges Frank M. Johnson and Seybourn H. Lynne listened attentively as Gray tried to explain why segregated busing violated the Fourteenth Amendment, which required states to provide equal protection under the law to all persons. Gray argued that ordering black citizens to the back of the bus, forcing them to stand over empty seats, and making them surrender their seats to white passengers was unconstitutional.

On June 4, the three judges announced their ruling. In a two-to-one majority decision (with Judge Lynne disagreeing), the court ruled that racially segregated seating on city buses was unconstitutional. Attorneys for Montgomery and the state of Alabama soon appealed the decision, meaning the bus/boycott situation would remain status quo indefinitely. Nevertheless, the announcement sparked a firestorm of celebration and hatred.

Meanwhile, segregationists branded southern judges Johnson and Rives as traitors. They bombarded them with hateful mail and phone calls for months. Moreover, a cross was burned on Johnson's lawn, and the gravesite of Rives' son was desecrated. Now in danger of losing the boycott war, the white establishment resorted to desperate measures. On August 25, the home of Robert Graetz, a white member of the MIA board, was bombed. More significantly, insurance companies canceled the automobile coverage of the volunteer taxi drivers. The city commissioners and White Citizens' Council members turned up the heat by pressuring southern insurance companies to refuse to cover the boycotters.

The agents themselves denied wrongdoing. Jim Upchurch, president of the Montgomery Association of Fire and Casualty Insurance Agents, called the claim "absolutely ridiculous. . . .

Robert Graetz speaking with King *(Courtesy of AP Images/Gene Herrick)*

But the car pool is a taxi-type operation and taxis always have trouble getting insurance." Luckily for the protesters, King found a black insurance agent in Atlanta, T. M. Alexander, who was able to contact Lloyd's of London. That internationally famous insurance company provided coverage for the protesters' fleet of vehicles.

In October, Mayor Gayle tried a new ploy. Through a state court, he sought a restraining order to prevent the boycotters from gathering on street corners. Their singing, he said, was a public nuisance. On November 13, the court was in the process of granting the order. But again, luck shone on the black citizens of Montgomery. For on that very day, the U.S. Supreme Court issued a decision—one that would stagger Jim Crow and empower everyone who believed in equal rights.

seven

Free at Last

The climactic triumph of the Montgomery bus boycott was like a scene from a Hollywood movie. On
November 13, 1956, Martin Luther King Jr. and other
boycott leaders fretted in a Montgomery courtroom. The city's
attorneys were trying to get Judge Eugene Carter to issue a
restraining order to prevent boycott participants from gathering on street corners. Moreover, the lawyers had testimony
that they hoped would convince the judge to shut down the
carpool system.

The attorneys argued that the boycott was not a willful
attempt by the masses to stay off the buses, but instead a private, moneymaking enterprise, which they insisted should be
banned or regulated. To support this, a witness testified that
the MIA had deposited $189,000 in a Montgomery bank.

But during the proceedings, a reporter handed a news bul-
letin to King. According to the Associated Press, King read,

the U.S. Supreme Court had just affirmed the lower court's ruling that had outlawed segregation on Montgomery's buses. The Supreme Court stated, succinctly: "The motion to affirm is granted and the judgment is affirmed." The Supreme Court cited the *Brown v. Board of Education* school segregation case of 1954 as well as subsequent decisions that outlawed segregation in public parks, on playgrounds, and on golf courses.

King quickly spread the news to his wife and friends, and soon the courtroom was abuzz. "God Almighty has spoken from Washington, D.C.!" someone shouted. The judge pounded his gavel and then issued the injunction against the carpool, but it all seemed irrelevant. A higher court had ruled on a broader, more fundamental issue.

Fred Gray, the MIA, and the determined black citizens of Montgomery had won the battle. The highest federal court had ruled that all segregation practices on the city's buses were illegal. Seats could no longer be reserved for whites, drivers could not ask black passengers to "give me those seats," and black citizens could enter through the front door just like everyone else. Should the city of Montgomery not obey the ruling, the federal government had the right to enforce the law.

Jo Ann Robinson, who had distributed the fliers at the start of the boycott on December 2, 1955, said:

> We felt that we were somebody. That somebody had listened to us, that we had forced the white man to give what we knew [was] our own citizenship. . . . And if you have never had the feeling that . . . you are [no longer] an alien, but that this is your country too, then you don't know what I'm talking about. It is a hilarious feeling that just goes all over you, that makes you feel that America is a great country and we're going to do more to make it better.

On the evening of November 13, the MIA staged a mass meeting to trumpet the good news. The jubilant crowd stood for King and showered him with applause. Women shouted for joy, and old men wept. The next day, MIA members unanimously voted to end the bus boycott once the U.S. Supreme Court decision was implemented.

Whites did not take kindly to the news. During a nighttime ride, dozens of Ku Klux Klansmen—dressed in costume—drove through black neighborhoods honking horns and shining lights into homes. On the legal front, white attorneys challenged the Supreme Court's decision, stating that it violated states' rights. However, the justices refused to hear their case. Their decision was final.

The days following November 13 proved to be among the toughest for the boycotters. The Supreme Court decision would not take effect until official orders were delivered to Montgomery, meaning bus segregation would continue until that time. Meanwhile, the injunction banning the taxi service went into effect. Thus, many black citizens were forced to walk long distances to work. King urged his followers to stick it out for the necessary few days. But those days turned into weeks, as Washington bureaucracy delayed the implementation.

Finally, the great day came. On December 20, on a day in which Mayor W. A. Gayle and Police Commissioner Clyde Sellers were out of town, U.S. marshals served the writs of injunction to the city of Montgomery. That evening, King asked some 1,200 boycotters to stand up if they were ready to return to the buses, now free from segregation. Joyously, they rose to their feet.

King insisted that black citizens behave nobly as they took their seats on the city buses. "No one goes on that bus tomorrow alone," King told the crowd. "Every Negro bears on his shoulders the weight of responsibility of the 50,000 Negroes in Montgomery. Violence must not come from any of us. For if we become victimized with violent intents, we will have walked in vain."

White leaders in Alabama knew that they had lost the bus segregation battle in Montgomery, but they were not giving up on the larger war. In response to the December 20 developments, Public Service Commission President Jack Owen sent telegrams to all bus companies in Alabama, outside of Montgomery, stating that they must continue to enforce segregation.

On December 21, black citizens desegregated Montgomery buses, ending a boycott that had lasted 381 days. At about seven o'clock on that morning, Forrest Castleberry, a white reporter for the *Montgomery Advertiser,* climbed aboard a

African Americans boarding a desegregated bus at the end of the boycott *(Courtesy of Don Cravens/Time Life Pictures/Getty Images)*

bus to write a firsthand account. The early-morning bus was mostly empty, but a middle-aged black man and a young black woman sat together—in the second row.

"Going to have a good Christmas?" he asked her.

"I hope so," she said.

At one point, King and his right-hand man in the boycott movement, Reverend Ralph Abernathy, boarded the bus together.

"Is this the reverend?" the driver asked politely.

"That's right," King answered. "How much?"

"Fifteen," the driver said.

King and Abernathy paid their fifteen-cent fares and sat down—Abernathy in the second row and King on the seat behind him. Joining them was a white minister named Glenn Smiley, field secretary of the Fellowship of Reconciliation, which was headquartered in New York City. "This is the largest demonstration of this sort of thing in the United States," Smiley told the reporter, "and is tremendously interesting to us."

At 7:20, King and Abernathy reached their destination and departed the bus.

"That was a might good ride," Abernathy said.

"It was a great ride," echoed King.

On December 21, 1956, King and Abernathy were among the first to ride on a desegregated Montgomery bus. Abernathy sits beside an unidentified woman, and King (second row) sits beside Glenn Smiley. *(Courtesy of AP Images)*

Rosa Parks sits toward the front of a Montgomery bus after the Supreme Court's decision outlawing segregation. *(Library of Congress)*

eight

Aftershocks

I n elementary school textbooks across America, children
learn the inspiring tale of Rosa Parks and the Montgomery
bus boycott. Typically, the story ends happily with bus
desegregation on December 21, 1956. Presumably, after that
date, everyone in Montgomery lived happily ever after. But
that's not at all how it happened. In the days and weeks following the boycott's conclusion, whites unleashed a wave of
violence against the city's black citizens.

On the buses, many whites seethed with anger. One elderly
white man stood in the crowded front end of a bus when he
could have sat down in the back. He explained that he "would
rather die and go to hell than sit behind a nigger." On another
bus, a white man slapped a black woman. "I could have broken
that little fellow's neck all by myself," the woman said later,
"but I left the mass meeting last night determined to do what
Reverend King asked."

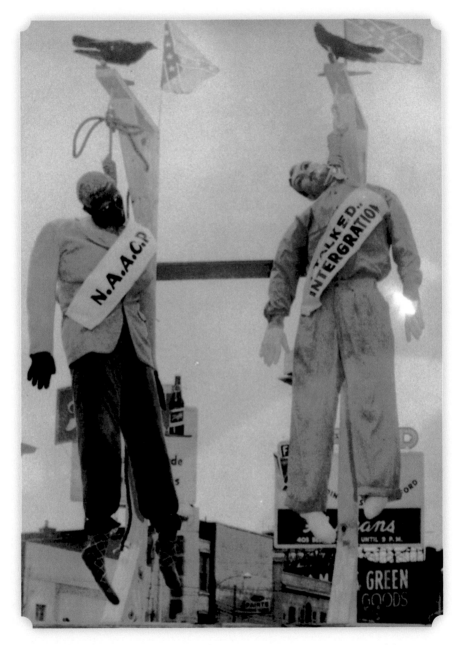

Two dummies hanged in downtown Montgomery in protest of bus integration *(Courtesy of AP Images)*

Early in the morning on December 23, 1956, someone fired a shotgun into the home of Martin Luther King Jr. Had King been standing in the wrong spot, he could have been killed. Though no one was hurt, King's father, "Daddy King," arrived later that day and demanded that his son refrain from any more activism. Tears were shed, prayers were offered, but Martin Jr. insisted that he continue serving his people.

The next day, as a fifteen-year-old black girl waited at a Montgomery bus stop, five white men confronted her. They beat the teenager and then quickly fled the scene. On Christmas Day, the violence spread to Birmingham, Alabama's largest city. Reverend Fred Shuttlesworth, who had already announced his intention to lead a boycott of that city's segregated buses on December 26, was rocked by a dynamite blast outside his home's window. Much of the house was destroyed, but Shuttlesworth escaped unharmed. His followers' attempt to sit in the buses' white section led only to a mass arrest. "Bombingham," as the city came to be called, would remain strongly segregated well into the 1960s.

Meanwhile, white supremacists waged almost guerrilla warfare against Montgomery's African Americans. In black communities, snipers shot into buses. King urged authorities to take a stand against the shootings, but Commissioner Frank Parks's response was to suggest the suspension of bus service. White extremists would have considered that a victory. The sniping continued, and on New Year's Eve shots struck a pregnant black woman, Rosa Jordan, in both legs. For a while, bus service was suspended during nighttime hours. At one point, white segregationists incorporated the Rebel Club, whose purpose was to provide a whites-only transportation system.

On January 10, 1957, whites staged the worst attacks since the boycott drama had unfolded more than a year earlier. That day, a bomb exploded at a black church in Montgomery. Before the day was through, whites had bombed four African American churches as well as two houses, including those of Reverend Ralph Abernathy and white minister (and MIA member) Reverend Robert Graetz. The Bell Street and Mount Olive Baptist churches were almost completely destroyed. The financial damage was estimated in the tens of thousands of dollars, and the emotional damage was incalculable.

In the wake of the bombings, the city shut down bus service for several days. Black citizens wondered if their year of sacrifice had been for naught. Virulent fliers were circulated

Abernathy and another minister standing in front of Abernathy's bomb-damaged home *(Library of Congress)*

in black neighborhoods, and King was among the many who fell into low spirits. At one point during a mass meeting, he broke down. "Lord, I hope no one will have to die as a result of our struggle for freedom in Montgomery," he said, overcome with emotion. "Certainly I don't want to die. But if anyone has to die, let it be me." The crowd, in an uproar, shouted "no, no."

Perhaps the saddest story of the Montgomery bus boycott centered on Juliette Morgan. On January 5, Buford Boone, editor of the *Tuscaloosa News,* told a gathering of the White Citizens' Council that whites were to blame for the recent violence in Montgomery. Morgan, the white Montgomery librarian who had written letters of support of the boycott during its early stages, wrote a letter of praise to Boone. "You help redeem Alabama's very bad behavior in the eyes of the nation and the world," she wrote. "I had begun to wonder if there were any men in the state—any white men—with any sane evaluation of our situation here in the middle of the Twentieth Century, with any good will, and most especially with any moral courage to express it."

Boone asked Morgan if he could print her letter, and she agreed reluctantly (having been harassed due to her letter writing a year earlier). This time, reaction to her letter was even worse. Whites pestered her with hateful letters and phone calls and boycotted the library at which she worked. Teenagers taunted her, and a cross was burned in front of her house. Friends, neighbors, and colleagues ostracized her. Mayor W. A. Gayle even withheld municipal funding for the library in an effort to have her fired.

The emotional toll on Morgan was overwhelming. On July 15, 1957, she resigned from the library. That night, she swallowed a bottle of sleeping pills and left a note: "I am not going to cause any more trouble to anybody." Her mother found her dead the next morning.

In the early weeks of 1957, the terror campaign continued in Montgomery. On January 28, white extremists bombed the home of a black hospital worker as well as the People's Service Station and Cab Stand. Another person planted a hastily assembled bomb (twelve sticks of dynamite) on King's porch. Although it was found smoldering, it did not go off. Once again, a crowd gathered around King's home. "We must not return violence under any condition," King told them. "I know this is difficult advice to follow, especially since we have been the victims of no less than ten bombings. But this is the way of Christ; it is the way of the cross."

The FBI arrested seven men who were accused of the January 9 and 28 bombings. Their much-publicized trial, however, reminded some of the Emmett Till court case of 1955. The defense attorneys not only tried to prove their clients' innocence, but they argued that MIA members bombed the buildings in order garner sympathy from outsiders, who would respond with donations. At one point, King was called to the witness stand. He later wrote about the incident:

> For more than an hour I was questioned on things which had no relevance to the bombing case. The lawyers lifted statements of mine out of context to give the impression that I was a perpetrator of hate and violence. At many points they invented derogatory statements concerning white people, and attributed them to me. The men had signed confessions. But in spite of all the evidence, the jury returned a verdict of not guilty.

Fortunately, the January 28 bombings were the last noteworthy violent acts related to the Montgomery bus boycott.

As the weather warmed in 1957, bus integration proceeded smoothly. By midyear, the buses were running like they had in 1955—except that black riders got to sit where they pleased. Desegregation actually had eased the tensions on the buses. It wasn't long before blacks and whites were chatting together and sharing smiles. Bus drivers also were more relaxed, as they no longer were required to enforce segregation. As summarized by King, "The skies did not fall when integrated buses finally traveled the streets of Montgomery."

Nevertheless, racial tension continued in other aspects of Montgomery society. During the sit-in movement that swept the South in 1960 to help integrate lunch counters and other public facilities, some Alabama State students were arrested for trying to desegregate the Montgomery County courthouse's snack bar. In the face of political pressure against Alabama State, some teachers resigned—including WPC president Jo Ann Robinson.

In the aftermath of the boycott, many wondered what had happened to Rosa Parks. Unlike King, she did not rise to glory. Parks lost her job at the department store, and her husband, Raymond, quit his job due to friction at work about Rosa's case. Parks did continue to work for the movement, speaking at rallies in various cities. However, Rosa and Raymond felt uneasy in Montgomery. Whites phoned them with death threats, and they worried that their home would be bombed (like those of the MIA leaders).

In August 1957, the couple moved to Detroit to be close to Rosa's younger brother. A year later, Rosa got a job as a hostess at an inn at Hampton Institute in Virginia. But in 1959, she moved back to Detroit to be with her family. She worked as a seamstress for a few years before landing a job as a staff assistant for Congressman John Conyers (D-MI) in 1965. She worked for him for twenty-three years before retiring in 1988.

After the boycott began, Parks sometimes second-guessed her famous act of civil disobedience. "In fact," she wrote, "if I had let myself think too deeply about what might happen to me, I might have gotten off the bus."

Millions of African Americans were grateful that she had refused to surrender her seat. Her defiance started a domino reaction that became known as the civil rights movement.

Congressman John Conyers

nine

Montgomery Sparks the Movement

O n May 27, 1956, a bus driver in Tallahassee, Florida, ordered two black women to get up from their seat so that a white woman could sit down. The women, Carrie Patterson and Wilhemina Jakes, were students at Florida A&M University. They did get up from the seat, but they demanded a refund of their bus fare. The driver, who didn't like their attitude, called the police, who arrested the women.

News of the arrest spread like wildfire, and the students of Florida A&M responded by boycotting the buses. Within days, the rest of Tallahassee's black citizens joined them in protest. Reverend C. K. Steele led the movement, which included a volunteer carpool system. "The issue is simply one of granting all American citizens who ride the public bus, regardless of race, the right to sit wherever they choose," Steele said.

The Ku Klux Klan reacted by burning crosses, while city authorities told the black community that it was sinful to deprive the city of its transportation system. But the boycotters refused to give in, forcing the bus company to suspend operations on July 1. Six months later, the City Commission repealed the bus company's segregation clause because of a recent federal ruling that had outlawed segregated buses

A college student hitchhikes during the Tallahassee bus boycott. *(Courtesy of AP Images)*

in Florida. The Inter-Civic Council ended the boycott on December 3, 1957.

The events in Tallahassee illustrate the impact that the Montgomery boycott had on the rest of the nation. Patterson, Jakes, and the rest of Tallahassee's black community had been inspired by the success in Montgomery. Moreover, the Supreme Court ruling that had banned segregated buses in Montgomery blasted the hopes of white leaders in Tallahassee. After Montgomery, African Americans across the South realized that they could whip Jim Crow if they worked together, persevered, and committed themselves to nonviolent protest.

Early in 1957, black leaders formed the Southern Leadership Conference on Transportation and Nonviolent Integration. Its name would evolve into the Southern Christian Leadership Conference (SCLC). According to the organization's official Web site, "The very beginnings of the SCLC can be traced back to the Montgomery Bus Boycott." On January, 10, 1957, the very day that Reverend Ralph Abernathy's house was bombed in Montgomery, leaders of the MIA and other protest groups met in Atlanta. "They issued a document," states the SCLC's site, "declaring that civil rights are essential to democracy, that segregation must end, and that all Black people should reject segregation absolutely and nonviolently."

In February 1957, SCLC members elected an executive board of directors that looked like a Who's Who of bus boycott leaders. MIA leaders Martin Luther King Jr. and Abernathy were elected president and financial secretary-treasurer, respectively. Reverend C. K. Steele, leader of the Tallahassee bus boycott, was elected vice president. And Reverend T. J. Jemison, who had organized the bus boycott in Baton Rouge in 1953, was elected secretary.

Under the charismatic leadership of King, who had risen to fame during the Montgomery boycott, the SCLC was a driving force of the civil rights movement. The organization helped stage a campaign against segregation in Albany, Georgia, in 1961-62. Thousands of African Americans participated, and hundreds were arrested.

In 1963, an SCLC desegregation campaign in Birmingham, Alabama, garnered international sympathy for the black cause. Public Safety Commissioner Bull Connor ordered

Ralph Abernathy (left) and Martin Luther King Jr. lead a group of demonstrators as they march toward the city hall in Birmingham. *(Courtesy of AP Images/Horace Cort)*

fire fighters to blast black protesters with fire hoses. He also encouraged police officers to bring out attack dogs. "I want to see the dogs work," Connor said. "Look at those niggers run." The world was appalled.

The SCLC was among several organizations involved in 1963's March on Washington. A racially mixed crowd of 250,000 heard King deliver the most famous American speech of the twentieth century. Near the culmination of the speech, King referenced the state in which the Montgomery boycott had occurred: "I have a dream that one day, down in Alabama, with its vicious racists, with its governor having his lips dripping with the words of interposition and nullification; one day right there in Alabama, little black boys and black girls will be able to join hands with little white boys and white girls as sisters and brothers."

The Birmingham campaign, the March on Washington, and King's "I Have a Dream" speech contributed tremendously to the passage of the 1964 Civil Rights Act. The act was designed to end segregation once and for all in the United States. Signed into law on July 2 by President Lyndon Johnson, the act banned discrimination in places of public accommodations, barred unequal voter registration requirements, and gave the U.S. attorney general more power to file lawsuits in order to protect citizens against discrimination. The law also required the elimination of discrimination in federally assisted programs, established the Equal Employment Opportunity Commission (EEOC), and authorized the commissioner of education to help communities desegregate schools.

While King and the SCLC—two direct connections to the Montgomery Improvement Association—helped destroy Jim Crow, the credit also goes to the thousands of black Southerners who stood up for justice. The defiance of Rosa

Parks, the courage of Montgomery's boycotters, the praise that the media bestowed on Montgomery's heroes, and the support of the U.S. Supreme Court—all of this emboldened black Southerners to fight for their rights.

On February 1, 1960, inspired by Rosa Parks, four black college students—Ezell Blair, David Richmond, Joseph McNeil, and Franklin McCain—sat at a whites-only lunch counter at Woolworth in Greensboro, North Carolina. A waitress refused them service, but the next day they returned with about two dozen "sit-in" protesters. The sit-in movement spread like wildfire throughout the South. By the end of the year, hundreds of students had been arrested or expelled for participating in such demonstrations. Yet their efforts were hugely successful. Establishments throughout the South began to desegregate their lunch counters.

The sit-in movement might never have happened were it not for the Montgomery bus boycott. Explained McNeil: "I was from North Carolina but I had lived in New York and when I went back down there to school I realized the transition, the difference in public accommodations. . . . It seemed to me that people in Alabama, where they had the Montgomery bus boycott, were at least trying to do something about it. The people in Little Rock, with the trouble at Central High School [in 1957], were trying to do something. And we weren't."

The sit-in movement also inspired southern black college students to form the Student Nonviolent Coordinating Committee (SNCC). The brave people of SNCC risked their lives to help black Southerners register to vote. They also contributed heavily to some of the pivotal campaigns of the civil rights movement. In 1961, SNCC leader John Lewis was among the many who were beaten and clubbed during the Freedom Rides. The Freedom Riders, who were mostly members of the Congress of Racial Equality, tried to desegregate interstate buses and facilities.

During 1964's Freedom Summer, SNCC members overcame shootings and bombings to register black voters in the state of Mississippi. In Selma, Alabama, in 1965, protesters were clubbed and tear-gassed on Bloody Sunday as they tried to march for voting rights. Their Selma to Montgomery march that spring was the pinnacle of the civil rights movement. On March 25, in front of a crowd of 50,000, King spoke about how the movement had started and ended in Alabama's state capital. "From Montgomery to Birmingham, from Birmingham to Selma, from Selma back to Montgomery, a trail wound in a circle and often bloody, yet it has become a highway up from darkness."

The Selma to Montgomery march inspired passage of another pivotal piece of legislation. The 1965 Voting Rights Act dramatically reduced the obstacles that had prevented African Americans from registering to vote. In many historians' eyes, it also marked the end of the civil rights movement. To King's dismay, more militant black-rights groups emerged in the late 1960s, including a radicalized SNCC as well as the Black Panthers. These groups abandoned the nonviolent principles that had made the Montgomery bus boycott so successful. King himself was felled by an assassin's bullet on April 4, 1968.

Though Rosa Parks participated in the 1965 Selma marches, she mostly kept a low profile for the rest of her long life. Only in old age did she seem to attract substantial national attention. In 1992, she published *Rosa Parks: My Story,* an autobiography that has become a staple of school libraries throughout the country. Three years later, she penned

Marchers cross the Edmund Pettus Bridge on their way from Selma to Montgomery in 1965. *(Library of Congress)*

Lyndon Johnson signs the Civil Rights Act of 1964. *(Library of Congress)*

the memoir *Quiet Strength*. In 1999, at age eighty-six, Parks was awarded the Congressional Medal of Freedom—the nation's highest civilian award—and that same year *Time* magazine named her one of the twenty most influential and iconic figures of the twentieth century.

Parks, however, remained humble throughout her life. Joseph Lowery, an activist in the civil rights movement, recalled that Parks gave his daughter a $25 check as a wedding present. After a year had passed and she still hadn't cashed the check, the daughter ran into Parks.

"Young lady," Parks told her, "why don't you cash that check? I can't get my bank account straight."

"Mrs. Parks, I will never cash that check," she responded. "It's a treasure to me to have this from you."

Recalled Lowery: "Mrs. Parks didn't understand it because

she didn't recognize her own place in history, and she left my daughter fussing, 'Young lady, cash that check.' That was the humility that hallmarked the life and ministry of Rosa Parks."

In 1990, Parks was invited to a ceremony in honor of Nelson Mandela, who recently had been released from prison. For twenty-seven years, Mandela had been incarcerated in South Africa for his defiant activism against apartheid in his country. Mandela spotted Parks in the reception line and gave her a hug. He said to her, "You sustained me while I was in prison all those years."

Rosa Parks died on October 24, 2005, at the age of ninety-two. On the day of her funeral, flags in Montgomery, Alabama—and all across America—were flown at half-mast, a final honor for the modest woman whose courage changed the world.

timeline

1865	The Thirteenth Amendment abolishes slavery.
1866	Southern states begin to enact "black codes" to subjugate African Americans.
1870	Tennessee passes a transportation segregation law—the first of many such laws in the South.
1896	The U.S. Supreme Court rules that it is constitutional for governments to maintain segregated facilities for black and white citizens.
1905	Black citizens in Nashville boycott the segregated streetcars.
1946	Mary Fair Burks founds the Women's Political Council (WPC) in Montgomery to help local black citizens register to vote.
1953	Black citizens in Baton Rouge, Louisiana, stage a bus boycott.
1954	The U.S. Supreme Court declares segregation in public schools unconstitutional.
1955 **August 28**	Black teenager Emmett Till murdered by two white men in Mississippi.
December 1	Rosa Parks arrested on a Montgomery bus for violating the bus segregation laws;

E. D. Nixon convinces her to fight the case in court.

December 2   Jo Ann Robinson and other WPC members distribute leaflets calling for boycott of Montgomery's buses on Monday, December 5.

December 5   The one-day boycott a huge success, as bus ridership among African Americans is more than 90 percent below normal; Rosa Parks convicted of disorderly conduct and fined $10; the Montgomery Improvement Association (MIA), with Martin Luther King Jr. as president, is formed to facilitate the boycott, which black citizens want to continue until their demands are met.

December   MIA leaders organize a volunteer taxi service.

1956

January 9   Black attorney Fred Gray's boycott-ending proposal is turned down by Montgomery's city commissioners.

January 22   A fabricated story in the *Montgomery Advertiser* states that black leaders have agreed to end the boycott.

January 26   Martin Luther King Jr. arrested for speeding.

January 30   A bomb explodes on Martin Luther

King Jr.'s front porch.

February 1	Fred Gray files a lawsuit (*Browder* v. *Gayle*) in a U.S. district court.
February 22	Dozens of boycott leaders arrested for involvement in what a grand jury has ruled an illegal boycott.
March 22	Martin Luther King Jr. found guilty of violating the state boycott law and fined $500.
May 27	A bus boycott begins in Tallahassee, Florida.
June 4	In *Browder* v. *Gayle,* federal judges rule that the bus segregation laws in Montgomery are unconstitutional.
November 13	The U.S. Supreme Court upholds the *Browder* v. *Gayle* decision.
November 14	MIA members vote to end the bus boycott once the U.S. Supreme Court decision is implemented (which will be December 20).
December 21	For the first time, African Americans sit where they please on Montgomery's buses.
December 23– Jan. 28, 1957	Montgomery's black community is ravaged by shootings and bombings.
1957 January	Martin Luther King Jr. and other black southern leaders form the Southern Christian Leadership Conference.

Sources

CHAPTER ONE: "Are You Going to Stand Up?"

p. 13, "All right, you . . ." David J. Garrow, *Bearing the Cross: Martin Luther King, Jr., and the Southern Christian Leadership Conference* (New York: HarperCollins, 2004), 11.

p. 13, "Y'all better make . . ." Rosa Parks, *My Story* (New York: Dial Books, 1992), 115.

p. 13, "Look woman, I . . ." "The Narrative of Rosa Parks," *Black Collegian*, http://www.black-collegian.com/african/rosaparks.shtml.

p. 13, "No, I'm tired . . ." Ibid.

CHAPTER TWO: Jim Crow's Stranglehold

p. 15, "Back then, we . . ." "Standing Up for Freedom," Academy of Achievement, http://www.achievement.org/autodoc/page/par0bio-1.

p. 16, "There were cases . . ." Ibid.

p. 21, "[T]he day the . . ." Linda T. Wynn, "Nashville's Streetcar Boycott," Tennessee State University, http://www.tnstate.edu/library/digital/nashv.htm.

p. 21, "secure for all . . ." Clayborne Carson, primary consultant, *Civil Rights Chronicle: The African-American Struggle for Freedom* (Lincolnwood, Ill.: Legacy Publishing, 2003), 49.

p. 23, "In the whole . . ." Henry Hampton and Steve Fayer, *Voices of Freedom* (New York: Bantam Books, 1990), 18-19.

p. 24, "concerned lest their . . ." Richard Kluger, *Simple Justice* (New York: Vintage Books, 1977), 60.

p. 24, "White and Negro . . ." "Bloodstains on White Marble Steps," *Jackson Daily News,* May 18, 1954.

p. 25, "The black people . . ." Mamie Till-Mobley and Christopher Benson, *Death of Innocence* (New York: Random House, 2003), 237.

p. 25, "Someone asked Rosa . . ." James Janega and Matthew Walberg, "Mother focused nation on son's death," *Chicago Tribune,* January 7, 2003.

CHAPTER THREE: Primed for Protest

p. 27, "had never felt . . ." Jo Ann Robinson, *The Montgomery Bus Boycott and the Women Who Started It* (Knoxville: University of Tennessee Press, 1987), 15.

p. 28, "Get up from . . ." Ibid., 16.

p. 28, "My friends came . . ." Ibid.

p. 31, "Before the boycott . . ." Hampton and Fayer, *Voices of Freedom,* 25.

p. 31-32, "The Women's Political . . ." Robinson, *The Montgomery Bus Boycott and the Women Who Started It,* 36.

p. 32, "I got mad . . ." John White, "Daybreak of Freedom: The Montgomery Bus Boycott," *Alabama Review,* October 1999, http://findarticles.com/p/articles/mi_qa3880/is_199910/ai_n8859643.

p. 33, "Mayor Gayle, three . . ." Juan Williams, *Eyes on the Prize* (New York: Penguin Books, 1987), 62.

p. 33, "You ought to . . ." Ibid.

p. 36, "But the joy . . ." Robinson, *The Montgomery Bus Boycott and the Women Who Started It,* 32.

p. 36, "black, dirty brats . . ." Ibid.

p. 38, "to become a . . ." "Background," *Fred Gray,* http://www.fredgray.net/background.html.

p. 38, "I done paid . . ." Bruce J. Dierenfield, *The Civil*

Rights Movement (Harlow, Essex, UK: Pearson Longman, 2004), 42.

p. 39-40, "People always say . . ." Parks, *My Story,* 116.

p. 40, "Why do you . . ." Ibid., 117.

CHAPTER FOUR: The Boycott Begins

p. 43, "I ended up . . ." Hampton and Fayer, *Voices of Freedom,* 20-21.

p. 43, "Oh, the white . . ." Beth Bailey and David Farber, consultants, *The Fifties Chronicle* (Lincolnwood, Ill.: Legacy Publishing, 2006), 271.

p. 43, "If you think . . ." Taylor Branch, *Parting the Waters: America in the King Years, 1954-63* (New York: Simon and Schuster, 1988), 131.

p. 43, "Baby, we're going . . ." Hampton and Fayer, *Voices of Freedom,* 21.

p. 44, Another Negro woman . . . Randall Kennedy, "Martin Luther King's Constitution: a Legal History of the Montgomery Bus Boycott," *98 Yale Law Journal,* 999-1067, April 1989, http://academic.udayton.edu/race/02rights/Civilrights03b.htm.

p. 45, "Don't ride the . . ." David L. Lewis, *King: A Biography* (Champaign: University of Illinois Press, 1978), 52.

p. 47, "I was in . . ." "Montgomery Movement Begins," *The Autobiography of Martin Luther King Jr.,* http://www.stanford.edu/group/King/publications/autobiography/chp_7.htm.

p. 47, "Eagerly we waited . . ." Ibid.

p. 48, "Negro 'goon squads' . . ." Branch, *Parting the Waters,* 135.

p. 49, "You wanted your . . ." Catherine A. Welch, *Children of the Civil Rights Era* (Minneapolis: Carolrhoda Books, 2001), 13.

p. 53, "Brother Nixon, I'm . . ." Peter John Ling, *Martin Luther King, Jr.* (New York: Routledge, 2002), 41.

p. 54, "yes . . . that's right," Branch, *Parting the Waters,* 139.

p. 54, "And you know . . ." Ibid.

p. 54-55, "There comes a . . ." Ibid., 140.

p. 55, "Now let us . . ." Ibid.

p. 55, "We are not wrong . . ." Ibid., 140-41.

p. 55, "Reverend King prayed . . ." Hampton and Fayer, *Voices of Freedom,* 24.

p. 57, "If we granted . . ." Williams, *Eyes on the Prize,* 77.

CHAPTER FIVE: Breakdowns

p. 62, "The Negroes of . . ." "Juliette Hampton Morgan: A White Woman Who Understood," *Tolerance.org,* http://www.tolerance.org/teach/printar.jsp?p=0&ar=671&pi=apg.

p. 63, "black men were . . ." Robinson, *The Montgomery Bus Boycott and the Women Who Started It,* 89.

p. 65, "My feets is . . ." Branch, *Parting the Waters,* 149.

p. 66, "In effect, the . . ." Garrow, *Bearing the Cross*, 52.

p. 67, "We are fighting . . ." Ibid., 53.

p. 68, "Well, you know . . ." Hampton and Fayer, *Voices of Freedom,* 27.

p. 69, "no more discussions . . ." Robinson, *The Montgomery Bus Boycott and the Women Who Started It,* 119.

p. 69, "[T]here seems to . . ." Sarah Woolfolk Wiggins, *From Civil War to Civil Rights: Alabama, 1860-1960* (Tuscaloosa: University of Alabama Press, 1987) 503.

p. 70, "Get out, King . . ." Frederic O. Sargent, *The Civil Rights Revolution: Events and Leaders, 1955-1968* (Jefferson, N.C.: McFarland, 2004), 21.

p. 72, "I have nothing . . ." Donald H. Matthews, *Honoring the Ancestors: An African Cultural Interpretation of Black Religion and Literature* (New York: Oxford

University Press USA, 1988), 100.

p. 72, "It seemed as . . ." Ibid.

p. 74, "Don't get panicky . . ." Jonathan Schell, *The Unconquerable World: Power, Nonviolence, and the Will of the People* (New York: Macmillan, 2003), 247.

CHAPTER SIX: Battles in the Courts

p. 77, "demolition of automobiles . . ." Robinson, *The Montgomery Bus Boycott and the Women Who Started It,* 139.

p. 79, "for her own . . ." Carson, *Civil Rights Chronicle,* 135.

p. 80, "Whenever the condition . . ." Robinson, *The Montgomery Bus Boycott and the Women Who Started It,* 146.

p. 82, "We just took . . ." Ibid., 150.

p. 83, "Long live the . . ." Carson, *Civil Rights Chronicle,* 139.

p. 87-88, "absolutely ridiculous . . ." "Boycott Pool Denied Car Insurance Policies," *Montgomery Advertiser,* September 17, 1956, http://www.montgomeryboycott. com/insurance_denied.htm.

CHAPTER SEVEN: Free At Last

p. 90, "The motion to . . ." Bob Ingram, "Supreme Court Outlaws Bus Segregation," *Montgomery Advertiser,* November 14, 1956, http://www.montgomeryboycott. com/segregation_outlawed.htm.

p. 90, "God Almighty has . . ." Branch, *Parting the Waters,* 193.

p. 90, "We felt that . . ." Williams, *Eyes on the Prize,* 88.

p. 91-92, "No one goes . . ." Edward Pilley, "Bus Desegregation Order Served Here: Negroes Vote to Call off Boycott Today," *Montgomery Advertiser,* December 21, 1956, http://www.montgomeryboycott.com/boycott_off. htm.

p. 93, "Going to have . . ." Ibid.

p. 93, "Is this the . . ." Ibid.

p. 93, "This is the . . ." Ibid.

p. 93, "That was a . . ." Ibid.

CHAPTER EIGHT: Aftershocks

p. 95, "would rather die . . ." Stephen B. Oates, *Let the Trumpet Sound: A Life of Martin Luther King, Jr.* (New York: HarperCollins, 1982), 107.

p. 95, "I could have . . ." Ibid.

p. 99, "Lord, I hope . . ." "The Expanding Struggle," *The Autobiography of Martin Luther King Jr.*

p. 99, "no, no . . ." Ibid.

p. 99, "You help redeem . . ." Mary Stanton, "Juliette Hampton Morgan," *Alabama Heritage,* Summer 2004, http://findarticles.com/p/articles/mi_qa4113/is_200407/ai_n9418232/pg_3.

p. 99-100, "I am not . . ." "Juliette Hampton Morgan: A White Woman Who Understood," *Tolerance.org,* http://www.tolerance.org/teach/printer.jsp?p=0&ar=671&pi=apg.

p. 100, "We must not . . ." James H. Cone, *Risks of Faith: The Emergence of a Black Theology* (Boston: Beacon Press, 1999), 58.

p. 100, "For more than . . ." "The Expanding Struggle," *The Autobiography of Martin Luther King Jr.*

p. 101, "The skies did . . ." Ibid.

p. 102, "In fact if . . ." Parks, *My Story,* 116.

CHAPTER NINE: Montgomery Sparks the Movement

p. 103, "The issue is . . ." Carson, *Civil Rights Chronicle,* 144.

p. 105, "The very beginnings . . ." "Our History," SCLC, http://www.sclcnational.org/net/content/page.

aspx?s=25461.0.12. 2607.

p. 105, "They issued a . . ." Ibid.

p. 106, "I want to . . ." Carson, *Civil Rights Chronicle,* 228.

p. 107, "I have a . . ." "The I Have a Dream Speech," *U.S. Constitution Online,* http://www.usconstitution. net/dream.html.

p. 108, "I was from . . ." Carson, *Civil Rights Chronicle,* 179.

p. 109, "From Montgomery to . . ." Clayborne Carson, et al., *The Eyes on the Prize Civil Rights Reader* (New York: Viking, 1991), 225.

p. 111, "Young lady, why . . ." "Remembering Rosa Parks," *Online NewsHour,* October 25, 2005, http://www. pbs.org/newshour/bb/race_relations/july-dec05/parks_ 10-25.html.

p. 112, "You sustained me . . ." Ssuna Ambrose Allan, "We can die but still live," *British Council InterAction,* May 24, 2007, http://www.bc-interaction.org/past_ events/cultural_heritage/articles/we_can_die_but_ still_live.

Bibliography

Allan, Ssuna Ambrose. "We can die but still live." *British Council InterAction*, May 24, 2007, http://www.bc-interaction.org/past_events/cultural_heritage/articles/we_can_die_but_still_live.

Bailey, Beth, and David Farber, consultants. *The Fifties Chronicle*. Lincolnwood, Ill.: Legacy Publishing, 2006.

"Bloodstains on White Marble Steps." *Jackson Daily News,* May 18, 1954.

"Boycott Pool Denied Car Insurance Policies." *Montgomery Advertiser,* September 17, 1956, http://www.montgomeryboycott.com/insurance_denied.htm.

Branch, Taylor. *Parting the Waters: America in the King Years, 1954-63.* New York: Simon and Schuster, 1988.

Brinkley, Douglas. *Rosa Parks: A Life.* New York: Penguin, 2005.

Carson, Clayborne, et al. *The Eyes on the Prize Civil Rights Reader.* New York: Viking, 1991.

———, primary consultant. *Civil Rights Chronicle: The African-American Struggle for Freedom.* Lincolnwood, Ill.: Legacy Publishing, 2003.

Cone, James H. *Risks of Faith: The Emergence of a Black Theology.* Boston: Beacon Press, 1999.

Dierenfield, Bruce J. *The Civil Rights Movement.* Harlow, Essex, UK: Pearson Longman, 2004.

Garrow, David J. *Bearing the Cross: Martin Luther King, Jr., and the Southern Christian Leadership Conference.* New York: HarperCollins, 2004.

———, ed. *The Walking City: The Montgomery Bus Boycott, 1955-1956.* New York: Carlson, 1989.

Gray, Fred. *Bus Ride to Justice: Changing the System by the System.* Montgomery, Ala.: River City, 1994.

———. "Background." *Fred Gray*, http://www.fredgray.net/background.html.

———, et al. *The Children Coming On . . .: A Retrospective of the Montgomery Bus Boycott.* Montgomery, Ala.: Black Belt Press, 1998.

Hampton, Henry, and Steve Fayer. *Voices of Freedom.* New York: Bantam Books, 1990.

Ingram, Bob. "Supreme Court Outlaws Bus Segregation." *Montgomery Advertiser,* November 14, 1956, http://www.montgomeryboycott.com/segregation_outlawed.htm.

Janega, James, and Matthew Walberg. "Mother focused nation on son's death." *Chicago Tribune,* January 7, 2003.

"Juliette Hampton Morgan: A White Woman Who Understood." *Tolerance.org,* http://www.tolerance.org/teach/printar.jsp?p=0&ar=671&pi=apg.

Kennedy, Randall. "Martin Luther King's Constitution: a Legal History of the Montgomery Bus Boycott." *98 Yale Law Journal* (April 1989): 999-1067. http://academic.udayton.edu/race/02rights/Civilrights03b.htm.

King, Martin Luther, Jr. *Stride Toward Freedom.* New York: HarperCollins, 1987.

———, and Clayborne Carson. *The Autobiography of Martin Luther King, Jr.* New York: Grand Central Publishing, 2001.

Kluger, Richard. *Simple Justice.* New York: Vintage Books, 1977.

Lewis, David L. *King: A Biography.* Champaign: University of Illinois Press, 1978.

Ling, Peter John. *Martin Luther King, Jr.* New York: Routledge, 2002.

Matthews, Donald H. *Honoring the Ancestors: An African Cultural Interpretation of Black Religion and Literature.* New York: Oxford University Press USA, 1988.

Oates, Stephen B. *Let the Trumpet Sound: A Life of Martin Luther King, Jr.* New York: HarperCollins, 1982.

Parks, Rosa. *My Story.* New York: Dial Books, 1992.

Pilley, Edward. "Bus Desegregation Order Served Here: Negroes Vote to Call off Boycott Today." *Montgomery Advertiser,* December 21, 1956, http://www. montgomeryboycott.com/boycott_off.htm.

"Remembering Rosa Parks." *Online NewsHour*, October 25, 2005, http://www.pbs.org/newshour/bb/race_relations/ july-dec05/parks_10-25.html.

Robinson, Jo Ann. *The Montgomery Bus Boycott and the Women Who Started It.* Knoxville: University of Tennessee Press, 1987.

Sargent, Frederic O. *The Civil Rights Revolution: Events and Leaders, 1955-1968.* Jefferson, N.C.: McFarland, 2004.

Schell, Jonathan. *The Unconquerable World: Power, Nonviolence, and the Will of the People.* New York: Macmillan, 2003.

Stanton, Mary. "Juliette Hampton Morgan." *Alabama Heritage,* Summer 2004, http://findarticles. com/p/articles/mi_qa4113/is_200407/ai_n9418232/pg_3.

Till-Mobley, Mamie, and Christopher Benson. *Death of Innocence.* New York: Random House, 2003.

Welch, Catherine A. *Children of the Civil Rights Era.* Minneapolis: Carolrhoda Books, 2001.

White, John. "Daybreak of Freedom: The Montgomery Bus Boycott." *Alabama Review,* October 1999, http:// findarticles.com/p/articles/mi_qa3880/is_199910/ ai_n8859643.

Wiggins, Sarah Woolfolk. *From Civil War to Civil Rights: Alabama, 1860-1960.* Tuscaloosa: University of Alabama Press, 1987.

Williams, Donnie. *The Thunder of Angels: The Montgomery Bus Boycott and the People Who Broke the Back of Jim Crow.* Chicago: Lawrence Hill Books, 2007.

Williams, Juan. *Eyes on the Prize.* New York: Penguin Books, 1987.

Web sites

http://www.montgomeryboycott.com
A video introduction, timeline, voices of the boycott, archived newspaper articles, and biographies of people who led the boycott are all featured on this superb site by the *Montgomery Advertiser*, a local newspaper in Montgomery.

http://www.pbs.org/wgbh/amex/eyesontheprize/story/02_bus.html
PBS maintains this excellent interactive site on the "Story of the Civil Rights Movement." It includes music, a video, a photo gallery, and even access to fliers circulated by the Montgomery Improvement Association on the eve of their victory, in addition to a lengthy article on the central role of singing at the Montgomery mass meetings.

http://www.africanaonline.com/montgomery.htm
This Web site on black American history summarizes the Montgomery boycott and provides links to related civil rights articles.

Index